Y0-BGF-960

# We Grow Up Fast Nowadays

**Also by**
**Jeffrey Artenstein**

*Runaways: In Their Own Words: Kids Talking About Living on the Streets*

Conversations with A New Generation

# We Grow Up Fast Nowadays

Jeffrey Artenstein

LOWELL HOUSE
Los Angeles

CONTEMPORARY BOOKS
Chicago

Library of Congress Cataloging-in-Publication Data

Artenstein, Jeffrey.
We grow up fast nowadays : conversations with a new generation / Jeffrey Artenstein.
p. cm.
ISBN 0-929923-46-4
1. Youth—United States—Attitudes. 2. Youth—United States—Interviews. 3. United States—Social conditions—1980. I. Title.
HQ796.A74 1991
305.23'5'0973—dc20 91-19604
CIP



Requests for such permissions should be addressed to:
Lowell House
1875 Century Park East, Suite 220
Los Angeles, CA 90067
Interior Design: Dan Kuffel
Manufactured in the United States of America

10 9 8 7 6 5 4 3 2 1

# Acknowledgments

Special thanks to:

June Kloubec and Erick Almond; Gale Wagnar—Gilreath and Randy Brazil; Dave Johnson; Tom Lazenby; Mark Costupoulos; Laura Fisher; John C. Jones; Adam Seitz; Kathy Harshburger; Dick Artenstein; Heidi Martrindale; Sandy Tattersall; Kelly Johnson; Leland Frommer; Jesper Sand; Cindy Franks; Linda White: Aase Neumann; Paul and Dina Radcliffe; Sharon Gazzo; Don Grimsrud; Rick Detorie; Jill West; Ruth and Oscar Brownstein; Nancy and Jack.

L. Spencer Humphrey, Janice Gallagher, Lise Wood, Patti Cohen, and the rest of the Lowell House staff.

The Boys and Girls Clubs of Minneapolis and Portland, Oregon; Atlantic High School of Delray Beach, Florida; the YWCA of Minneapolis; the Peddie School in Hightstown, New Jersey; St. Joseph's School of Bristol, Connecticut.

# 1

# Engine Trouble

On March 10, 1990, I packed my car beyond capacity and headed east out of Los Angeles on I-40. I planned to relocate to New York, where a friend had invited me to stay while I looked for my own apartment.

On day two, when I hit the New Mexico border, my RPM gauge began to give off space-shuttle readings. The engine sputtered and failed, and I limped to the side of the road, a solitary figure in a vast desert landscape. I sat near the car, like a Levis commercial, for several hours before being towed to a service station in Gallup. The mechanic looked over my foreign car reluctantly. It took him three minutes to find the dip stick.

"Can't do nothin'."

"Why not?"

"Gotta bring it to the Goodyear place down the road. They got a mechanic over there knows about foreign cars."

"How am I gonna get down the road?"

"Push it. But you better push fast, they'll be closin' soon."

I walked out to the street to have a look. Two teenagers, boy and girl, asked if I was going west, and if I was could they have a ride. They were a little ragged—the weary-eyed look you get from being on the road. I sympathized with them, but at the moment I wasn't going west—I wasn't going anywhere. I made an offer. "Help me push the car down the road, and I'll buy you dinner." They accepted, and we pushed toward the silhouette of the Goodyear blimp.

"Can't do nothin'."

"Why not?"

"Guy you want's gone for the night. Come back tomorrow around 12 and we should have some word on it."

So Eddy and Dorothy and I went to a little Tex-Mex restaurant, and as we ate chili and quesadillas, they told me their story. They were both 16, former high-school classmates from a suburb of Minneapolis on their way to Los Angeles to start their adult lives. One of them was pregnant.

Their families consented to the trip and to having the baby. They had given the kids money for bus fare and food. It was arranged that Eddy and Dorothy would stay with a relative in Orange County and that Eddy would go to work in a fruit-packing plant. They had left Minnesota one week before I met them.

Here is how they described their week on the road:

EDDY: We decided to make a vacation out of the trip. Instead of taking the bus, we cashed in the ticket and started hitching down I-35. We were gonna, like, use the money for cheap motels, take our time and see some things.

DOROTHY: Kinda like a last fling, you know, before we settle down in L.A. We had fun in Kansas City, walked around and stuff, and met this guy in a record store—he worked there—who made a dinner party for us, wine and everything.

EDDY: But it was tough gettin' outta there. We spent the whole day at a truck stop tryin' to get a ride. Eventually, this guy in a pickup drove us to Wichita. We were tired and didn't want to walk around, so we took this motel that was way too expensive, bought a lot of food and some wine and just stayed in there for like, 15 hours.

DOROTHY: So here we are. We can't afford a bus ticket, so we're gonna hitch to L.A. We've got enough for some food and cigarettes. (I offer to give them a few bucks.) No, we're OK. We made a mistake by blowing all the money—we gotta pay for it. We've gotta be responsible. I mean, I've got a baby on the way. In a way I guess it's good to make mistakes now, so we won't make them when Chris comes.

EDDY: It's unbelievable how fast the money goes. (Tactfully, I ask if it isn't a little early for them to settle down.) We're normal 16-year-olds. I mean, we know what's going on from experience. My father asked how we knew enough to be on our own. I told him that times have changed. There's five or six girls in school with babies—they're different than us, I mean, Dorothy and me've been together for three years. We wanna have a baby. But anyway, high school now is just like being an adult, there are drugs, gangs that'll kill you if you mess with 'em, sexual diseases . . . We grow up fast nowadays.

We talked about the food for a minute—great food, spiced to kill—then they thanked me. Dorothy said, "If you're ever in Minneapolis, try the hot buffalo wings at Rudolph's. You'll love 'em." They hoisted their bags and were gone.

Wanting nothing more in life than to wash I-40 out of my hair, I took a room at the El Rancho Hotel and Motel, "The Southwest's most enchanting hotel in the heart of Navajo land." Life-size Navajo mannequins scared the hell out of me when I turned corners in the lobby and corridor.

The next morning I got word that my distributor was shot and would be two days in repairing. During that time I thought a lot about Eddy and Dorothy. On the outside they were normal enough: Dorothy's long, blond hair tied in the back—still no sign of Chris—Eddy's Minnesota Gophers sweatshirt and Reeboks. What was odd, of course, was their determination to settle down and start a family at the age of 16. They were looking forward to it. And road-ragged as they were, I know they were enjoying their adventure thoroughly. But still, was she ready for a baby? She had chain-smoked Merits all through dinner. Was he ready to pack fruit? I wondered how extraordinary their story was. Most of all I wondered if their story in any way indicated the state of America's youth. How adultlike are today's kids? What are their concerns? What do they see as their problems, and how are those problems solved? Eddy's reflections stuck with me: "We're normal 16-year-olds . . . We grow up fast nowadays . . . It's unbelievable how fast the money goes."

I called my publisher from the El Rancho and proposed that, with the help of an advance, I drive the country over and record interviews with kids of all ages, however I found them, with a view toward discovering today's youth. My publisher agreed.

I had a head start. Two years earlier I had written a book called *Runaways,* a collection of stories about homeless kids, taken from interviews I conducted at a runaway shelter in Los Angeles. In the six months I spent there as a shelter supervisor, I came to know drug dealers, addicts, prostitutes, pimps—most of them in their midteens—who ran away, not for adventure, but to escape miserable lives of physical or psychological abuse. They did whatever they had to in order to survive.

I was 22 when I wrote that book, close enough to teenage culture and language to win the confidence of my interviewees. I learned how to turn interviews into conversations; I employed a combination of understanding, sensitivity, and entertainment. The kids told me things they would never have told an outsider, a jacket and tie.

In *Runaways,* I researched a very special, alienated group of kids. Now, I was going to use that experience to approach the subject of today's youth from the other side, by exploring an entire generation.

This was the beginning of a road trip that measured five months and 15,000 miles. I talked with more than 300 kids, ages 6 to 17, representing every religious, racial, and economic group. Their thoughts proved shocking, entertaining, mundane, and prophetic. I talked with kids in big cities and small towns, and I made copious notes, hoping to discern some link between region and personality. I opted to meet kids more or less by chance; I stayed far away from Mormons and pregnant girls and Indian reservations and rehab centers and Amish farms and runaways, because I didn't want to discover only stereotypes, to meet kids I already knew. I wasn't interested in conducting a survey. I hoped to create a forum where kids were free to speak their minds. I wanted my findings to be fresh and unsolicited.

I found the kids generally eager to talk, and in the end I concluded that Eddy was right. There is a new breed of American youth: a youth exposed to more extreme circumstances than previous generations; a youth with less supervision and greater independence and thus a broader perception; a youth of changed values. Today's kids face adult pressures and make adult decisions, but they are still kids, and this disparity often confuses them as well as their parents.

This book is not a survey or a scientific study. I didn't prod the kids you are about to meet, or pry into their personal lives. I set up my tape recorder and started talking—about anything. If I won their confidence, I steered the conversation in the direction of topics of interest to them, navigating by their enthusiasm and listening for clues to find the issue uppermost in their minds. Often I got mere bits and pieces—many times nothing at all. But sometimes they told me things they wouldn't have told their own parents, things that had been bubbling under the surface for a long time.

In the course of doing all this I became a creature of the road, staying in innumerable cheap motels and shaving in my rearview mirror. I saw famous landmarks and sat on back porches in deserted little one-road towns. I involved myself with the kids, their parents, and their towns, often staying a night or two as their guest. We talked and ate and drank, and often they insisted I see this or that, or visit friends of theirs in a neighboring state.

One of the wonderful things about traveling is the ease with which the traveler stumbles into the lives of strangers. In my five months I met three priests, two criminals, five police officers, an oil-rig driller, a brain surgeon, a professional baseball player, a 70-year-old school crossing guard, several writers and actors, a jazz musician, a fashion designer, a used-car salesman, a cartoonist, a couple of vagabonds, and a man who sold towels he swore had been used by the legends of Hollywood.

The morning after my dinner with Eddy and Dorothy, my new distributor and I left the El Rancho and drove northeast on 54, a miserable little two-lane, toward Wichita. It was a long drive. At about midnight, just outside of Wichita, the plastic roadside reflectors began to take on the shapes of giant farm animals, and I knew it was time to stop. Motel 6, a little sleep, eggs Benedict at Denny's, back in the car—a cycle I would come to know well.

I looked at my map and saw I was just a few miles from I-35, which goes straight to Minneapolis. I needed a place to settle down for a few weeks, to use as a testing ground, to determine, through practice, the best approach for arranging and conducting interviews with kids. I decided on Minneapolis partly because of Eddy and Dorothy. I had never been to Minnesota, but I rationalized that middle America—mid-American values, friendly people, and so on—would be a good starting point. I had a friend in Minneapolis, too, who would find me a place to stay. But as I drove north on I-35, the only thing on my mind was sitting down to a plate of the hot buffalo wings at Rudolph's. And that was the first thing I did when I arrived the next evening.

# 2

# Minneapolis, Minnesota

*I loved Minneapolis from the start. The town has a happy, cozy atmosphere that prompts you to look on the bright side. Instead of cursing the cold, I looked forward to getting inside and warming my hands by the fireplace—even though I didn't have one. Minnesotans are proud to be Minnesotans, and that's a very attractive trait. They are devoted to their local history, the local brews, and the local teams—even perennial losers like the Twins and Northstars.*

*It's a pretty state, the State of Ten Thousand Lakes, several of which are located in the Twin Cities themselves. My friend, Ali, arranged for me to stay with a friend of hers near Lake of the Isles. It was the first week of March, there was snow on the ground, and the lake was dotted with skaters; kids gathered and played hockey where snowplows had created a natural rink.*

*It was years since I had driven in snow, and I didn't like it. It was worse when the snow melted; I've never seen so many potholes in my life. I was told they result from the extreme climate: brutal cold in the winter, sweltering heat in the summer.*

*I found Minnesotans to be conservative, very polite, and unassuming. You can't place an operator-assisted call or buy a pack of chewing gum without first exchanging the requisite pleasantries:*

*"Hi, how are you?"*

*"Fine, thanks. And you?"*

*"Good. Little cold though. . . ."*

*Charming, up to a point, after which I began to buy my gum in the 20-pack economy size.*

*I learned the hard way that sarcasm is often met with blank faces. And I was scolded for referring to a 22-year-old female as a girl and not a woman. But it was all charming, in a way. As I started working I expected to find happy, healthy, innocent kids.*

*The first two weeks were a miserable failure. I couldn't seem to make contact with any kids at all. I expected to raise some eyebrows—these are not good times for working alone with kids, especially young ones—but it was worse than I anticipated. The public school system and three private schools denied me permission to interview their students. Administrators told me that a man had recently gone through the Minneapolis schools recruiting kids for a private music program. He molested one or more of them and was thrown in jail. Because of this, they predicted, I would be met with suspicion.*

*More days passed until finally the Uptown YWCA, after calling my publisher, granted me entrance to their after-school day-care program. Chaos and calamity; kids with wet chlorine hair were ricocheting off the walls, screaming and taking prisoners. These were all kids from "good" families, living in the picturesque uptown area.*

*I was a little nervous. I had no idea how I would go over, whether or not the kids would respond. My first interview was with Kelly, a bouncy seven-year-old with a runny nose. I wouldn't have to worry about her responding—she never shut up:*

Adults always have their way and kids never have theirs:

"Can you bring me out to get some ice cream?"

"No, I have to work."

"Mooooooom!"

"That's the way it always goes."

"Look how short my hair is. It used to be this long, but my dad said I had to get it cut. I didn't want to get it cut but he made me. I was racing with a friend of mine to see who could grow their hair out the fastest. My hair was always longer than hers—now look! I'm going to visit my dad next week. Let's just hope he doesn't make me cut my hair again!

My dad lives in Omaha. I have fun when I go to visit him—we go to the ice-cream store every night. But I have fun with my mom too. I like Minneapolis better than Omaha. There are no sidewalks in Omaha, and it bothers me because everywhere you go you have to walk on the side of the street. Then when people see you out on the grass they say, "Get off my grass!" What are you supposed to do?

I love Minneapolis. I've been to other places: Omaha, Bismarck . . . I like it here. When you come here it kinda clings on to you. It's cozy. But I've lived here all my life so I should like it. My mom's friend comes to visit and she says, "This is a real nice place to live but it's so cold in the winter and so hot in the summer." I like the snow because sometimes it gets more than a foot deep and you can do some real sledding. In the summer we swim in the lakes. You know, Minnesota has ten thousand lakes.

My favorite subject in school is science. I like Albert Einstein. Kids in my class who are interested in physics and stuff, they say he's a radical dude.

*What do you know about Albert Einstein?*

He was the one who put bubbles in beer.

*If you could meet any famous person, even one that's dead, who would it be? Einstein?*

Well, that might be a little boring. I'd rather meet the guys from New Kids on the Block.

*Who's the last person you'd like to spend the day with?*

Cheryl Whickly. I spend every day with her.

*Who's she?*

She's in my class. She whines over everything. She never stops crying.

*Would you like to meet the president?*

Not really. But if I did, and I could tell him anyone's name and have him give them a punishment, it would have to be Cheryl Whickly. (*Giggles.*) I have a boyfriend, you know, at school—I'm one of the only girls that does. He's eight years old and his name's Ted.

*How did you meet him?*

He was in my first-grade class, that's how I met him. This is kinda weird . . . my lips went to his cheek . . .

*What!?*

(*Quickly*) We bumped into each other. I was carryin' somethin' while I was reading it and I walked into him and my lips went to his cheek. (*Laughs.*) He's in a different class now. We don't get to talk at lunch, because this is one of those schools where you have to sit in a certain place, two tables for each class. (*Kelly has a cold, and she sneezes on my tape recorder.*) Sorry! (*Giggles.*) I talk to him on the bus. That's a nice tape recorder.

*I asked Jerry, eight, if there was anything that concerned him. He gazed out the window with pale blue eyes and dreamed as he spoke.*

Yes, because I want to be a marine biologist—I like the sea—and I know it's getting polluted. We don't have any ocean here, but we have ten thousand lakes.

I think that we should live like we did a few million, zillion years ago. If we did, we wouldn't be inventing cars that hurt the atmosphere. I take a special class about things like that. Every month we have a different subject. Last month we had recycling, and this month we have endangered species. My family recycles everything.

*(Jerry tilts his head down and looks me over through his bangs, fearing I'll find his next comment silly.)* I help endangered species, because whenever I see an animal for under $72 I buy it. I have $800 in the bank, and I use it to buy animals. My dad puts $100 in my bank every year for my birthday.

I'd also like it if I could someday stop pollution and execution. I think executing people is wrong; it's rotten and cruel and nasty and mean.

*Is execution legal here in Minnesota?*

I'm not sure, but if it is I'd like to stop it.

*One of the counselors sent in Lisa-Lynn, a 10-year-old, after telling me, "She's one of the few kids whose parents are still together. I know them well; they're the most energetic, creative parents I've ever met." The girl was beaming—full of life—and her freckles, her wide eyes, and her habit of twirling her black ponytail won me over.*

My family takes *big* vacations. I mean, when we go, it's a *vacation*. We went up to Split Rock Lighthouse, up by Duluth, last year. We got the best spot in the whole campground: number 13, even though it's an unlucky number. It has a path down to Lake Superior. And it has bears too, and we saw them. They weren't really big, but they were still bears. We rent a cabin every summer and we stay up in the woods. We go on long hikes—my dad always organizes 'em—we go fishing and everything. My dad's family does a lot of fishing, and my mom's family does a lot of hunting. I like fishing a lot—my dad has like 12 fishing rods. This year we had the first annual All-Huhart One-Day Ice-Fishing Tournament. That's what my dad named it. We're doin' it every year from now on. We were at Clearwater Lake. It was the whole family, and that's a lot 'cause there's like 10 on my mom's side and 10 on my dad's side. You should have seen Grandma and Grandpa Huhart. They're really lively, you know, my grandma goes running all the time and Grandpa still works all day long at the same place he always worked at. So anyway, my grandma, she was—you know those motored ice-augers—she was trying to cut the hole in the ice so we could start the tournament. And it's real hard to do, and she started spinning around with it *(giggles)*, and you know the way it keeps going down after it cuts through the ice? *(Giggles.)* Well, it kinda took Grandma with it. She didn't go through the ice or nothing—it had her like, pinned over the hole. She was like, "Help! Help!," and Grandpa was standing there laughing. *(Imitates her grandpa.)* "Help? Do you need help?"

*(She slides to the edge of her chair and, with frightening ease, folds her left leg around her neck as she continues excitedly. She remains folded for two or three minutes.)*

But you know what? Me and my dad were exploring the lake, and we found—this is gross, but—we found a dead dog. He probably froze. He had all these rotted areas, like a mummy or something, and his hind leg was like, off and everything. . . . No, things like that don't make me sick. But it was pretty gross. But aside from that, the trip was good. Most of our camping and fishing trips are a success.

We're making this big car trip this summer. We're driving from here to Virginia Beach. I'm gonna see the Capitol and the Lincoln Memorial when we go through Washington. In New York we'll see Central Park and the Statue of Liberty. Then we go down to Virginia Beach. It's like eight hours, or thirteen hours or something. We were planning it out a few days ago when we were watching the Gophers. So I'm looking forward to that. It'll be nice to see the ocean.

*Doesn't it bother you to sit in a car for that long?*

No, I don't have any brothers or sisters. If I did I probably wouldn't like it. But we play games and things—Hangman or whatever. We're bringing this humongous tent with us. We're gonna take our time and do a lot of camping. It's a big tent for three people, it has screen windows, there's room for a picnic table and everything.

*I'm a city person—I could never sleep in a tent. Don't you get, like, squirrels nibbling at your toes and mosquitos chewing on your eyelids?*

*Nooooo.* This tent'll keep out the bugs. We go to walk-in camps. That's where you go in and park your car in a lot. Then you walk over to the campground, so you don't have cars by the tents. They have these big wheelbarrows for you to roll your stuff over. We're always pretty comfortable when we're camping; we take walks around the campground and talk to the other people and . . . *Nooooo,* we *don't* go to nice restaurants! We make our own food! We grill steaks with a little grill and make baked potatoes and corn.

One time we were just sitting in our tent at night when the ranger came in. He goes, "Did you see that?" He told us a bear had just walked right behind our tent. Just like, an inch away!.

Am I talking too much? Well, anyway, try camping one time—come with us; we'll teach you everything.

*What a great kid! So warm and receptive, so full of life, such high color, such nice parents . . . So far, the young kids were just as I had expected: carefree and nonchalant.*

*Then came Ellen, a nine-year-old bundle of fraying nerves. Everything about her was unresolved, from her untied shoelaces to the three tufts of hair that shot up indiscriminately from the top of her head. This was no conversation; Ellen never recognized me as a person, only as an interviewer. She talked, I listened:*

*What's the story behind the Twin Cities? What's the difference between Minneapolis and St. Paul?*

Well, St. Paul's kinda like the place where someone goes if they want to commit a murder or rob a bank. St. Paul is full of all these big grocery stores, malls and everything. Bums hang out there. You shouldn't go there alone.

I like Minneapolis, but it's real big, you know. Every day there's a fire or a kid gets kidnapped or something. . . . Yeah, it does scare me, but when that happens I just think of something else. Like things that are nice: cartoons, school, my friends. My dad tells me—my mom and dad are divorced—not to walk alone. Not even here in Minneapolis. I just walk around my block. It looks really scary around here. I had my bike stolen once. Sometimes I'm scared that some guy, when he's walking by or bringing the mail around or whatever, that he's gonna take me away. My dad lives in Edina. There's no crime there.

*What would you change about the cities if you could?*

I'd find Jacob Wetterling and all the people who were kidnapped, and I'd bring them back. Then I'd find all the people that killed other people and put them in jail. And all that other stuff. *(Jacob Wetterling, age nine, was abducted in October 1989 in Minneapolis while he was riding his bike with two friends. A man approached the boys, asked them their ages, then forced Jacob into his car. The two other boys were left alone. A massive effort to find Jacob proved futile.)*

One time we were going out to dinner and we forgot to lock the door. When we came back we thought that somebody had broken into the house. Nobody really did. But when I went to sleep that night I was dreaming that there was this guy who was taking things. I had six dollars and I was sayin', "I'll give you six dollars if you quit." And he goes, like, "I want more! I want more!" And my mom was just sittin' there—she wasn't doin' anything—"Oh, hi, honey. How are you doing?" She was just relaxing when this burglar was in the house. It was weird.

My parents have been divorced ever since I was little. My dad is a broker and my mom works for AIDS. She tells everyone what's going on with it and how you can avoid it.

I don't have any brothers and sisters. Sometimes I wish I did. But I have friends I can play with and stuff.

I don't really get along with boys. They're all excited about Mutant Ninja Turtles and Bart Simpson and all that. There was one boy who sent a rose to a girl in my class. I wouldn't mind getting a rose, but I wouldn't, like, give him anything back. I'd just take the flower.

*(I remain quiet. Ellen looks right through me and continues answering questions I haven't even asked.)*

I never really get to see my dad that much anymore. Every other weekend I'm with my dad and the rest of the time I'm with my mom. It's weird because I'm only with my dad for four days a month. But I'm going with him for two weeks when I have vacation.

He has a girlfriend—she cooks every morning and every night! We make cakes in the morning without even planning it out! My mom doesn't cook. And that's not good because there are too many places to eat in Minneapolis. You can't choose which one. And when I do, my mom's like, "That one has too much grease; that doesn't have your vegetables." With her it's all TV dinners. She doesn't even know if I like roast or not. . . . No, no, she has time but she just doesn't do it. She never cooks anything unless someone helps her. So I decide I'll cook for myself and she goes, "Well, we can't go to the market to get that cottage cheese." I have my own cookbook from the last day-care program I was in. We used to cook a lot. But she won't let me cook anything. We have a thousand cookbooks in the house, but we never cook anything! We have little bugs in the kitchen. Whenever we go to get the Tupperware things from the cabinet, all these little bugs crawl out.

My dad's girlfriend is a great cook. She's nice and everything, but he'll never marry her. He would think that it would be hard on me. That's good. I don't want him to get married. She couldn't be my boss like my mom is. I mean, one time she said, "You shouldn't go outside 'cause it's too cold outside," and I said, "No it isn't." We had an argument and everything but I went outside anyway, 'cause I'm really with my dad. She doesn't really have anything to do with me. I just went outside.

*(She sighs and delivers her final paragraph in one long exhalation.)*

I've been in after-school programs for a long time. I just wanna go home, but my mom says I'm not old enough. I mean, everybody's talking about Teenage Mutant Ninja Turtles—my cousins get to go home and watch it, and Chip and Dale and all that. But I never get to watch it. There's no TV here. We're always moving here—swimming, running . . . Yeah, it is fun, but it gets boring after a while. Sometimes I don't feel like swimming. I'd rather lie down and watch TV.

*Are you having fun being a nine-year-old?*

Mmmm . . . I liked it better when I was eight.

*I was having fun with these kids, but Ellen left me tired and doubtful. She was my first adult-child, and she shocked me. How could a nine-year-old know so much stress?*

*In the coming months I would see a lot of fear, anger, stress, and pathos such as Ellen's. The Jacob Wetterling case came up again and again at the YWCA, and I heard about similar cases in other cities; for some kids the fear of abduction is ever-present. Another girl at the Y said, "When you're walking down the street, you never know. There's always a chance one of the cars will stop, and someone'll snatch you up."*

*Erik, another counselor at the Y, told me about an old hockey buddy of his who ran a college ice rink, and his daughter, Kay, an up-and-coming figure skater. He described their relationship as unique: "He doesn't worry about her. He doesn't watch over her, lecture her. He trusts her completely, and she's never done anything to break his trust. She's the perfect kid."*

*The next day Erik and I joined a pickup game at the rink. I met Kay's father on the ice. He was a great skater and still boyish looking with his shiny face and short, spiky hair. I met Kay at the ice rink one week later. She was a picture of Minnesota: light hair, blue eyes—she had just come off the ice and her cheeks were flushed. We sat in the referees' changing room and talked for an hour.*

My dad was a real good hockey player in high school. I guess that's how he started here. He's been working here for 15 years; now he's in charge. Our whole family knows the ice.

I've been skating most of my life. I started taking lessons when I was four years old. I started skating seriously, every day, about five years ago, when I was nine. I've been out there *(she points to the rink)* just about every day since then, winter and summer. I have two coaches—they're real good—and I skate about four, sometimes five and a half hours a day. I skate mornings before school three times a week. I'm up at 4:30 and I'm here at 5:30. I skate for an hour, and I'm at school at 7. I get out of school at 1:50, and my dad picks me up and brings me right back here. It's nice because my dad and I both work in the same place. I skate from 2:45 to 6:45. I'm pretty busy. I skate only one day on the weekends, so I do have a day off.

I also take an edges class, which stresses grace and gliding. I really like that class, 'cause it makes you feel like a kid again. You deal with the basics instead of getting right into double jumps and everything.

I'm not so much a competitive skater as a "test" skater. I skate for the tests. I'm on my gold in figures, and I have two more freestyle tests to pass. The tests are like belts in karate. You have to pass these tests to compete on certain levels; like Jill Trenary *(the current world champion singles skater and a Minnesotan)* had to get her gold to compete as a senior for the Olympics. There are nine tests and then you have the gold. Then you can teach and everything. It's real important to me. I'm going for my gold next month.

I do maybe one or two competitions a year. I don't like the way jumping means everything in competition. You can be a great skater and skate beautifully, but if you miss that double . . . Getting my gold is my real goal. More than that though, I do it 'cause I love it. It's something that I can do for the rest of my life. I never regret all the time I've spent on the ice. I know it's worth it. It's a great feeling I get when I pass a test; it's a real accomplishment. It's given me a higher self-confidence, because I see myself working and improving all the time. I love doing figures—that's when you trace over the figure eight. I love trying to make things as perfect as I can. I'm not the best jumper in the world. I've got a good lay-back spin, I get a lot of compliments on that.

*(Kay leans back in her chair and smiles. She is all-confident. Perhaps she is imagining this interview is taking place at the '92 Olympic Games.)*

Sometimes I think about skating in school. I'll be sitting in algebra and I'll think, "Wow, I'd really love to do an axel right now." I'd like to go professional—get into a show or teach or something—but I also want to go to college very badly.

My brother's a hockey player. He's real good, he plays in high school. My dad's *extremely* good. He knows what's going on out there. It's nice that the family likes the ice and that my dad manages the rink. I get a lot of extra ice. The hour I get in the morning is free. In the summer it's my dad who runs the program, so we get all that ice free. He likes being here too, but I don't think he gets paid what he's worth. He makes jokes about it. But, my brother goes to a very expensive school, and I have these coaches . . . it's like he works to give us what we want.

I don't think that the art of figure skating is *that* high on my dad's list, but he likes it because he knows I enjoy it. He encourages me. I know he doesn't like some of the figure-skating people because he thinks they're stuck up. He puts up with them, but he doesn't enjoy it. They always have to have everything the way they want it. I try to stay away from it. Coaches and skaters and hockey players were always like, "Go tell your dad . . . Bring this home to your dad." The manager's daughter.

*Your dad seems to be a fixture around here.*

He is. Everyone knows him and everyone likes him. He puts in so much extra time and work. He doesn't get paid for what he's worth.

I think I have a better relationship with my dad than most teenagers do. We're both here during the day; he comes to pick me up at school—"How was school? How was skating?"

*At this point Kay's father came in. I asked him how he felt about Kay's devotion to skating:*

From a parent's standpoint I think it's great that Kay spends so much time on the ice. She's not hanging around with her friends doing nothing or getting into trouble like so many other kids, and she still has time to socialize at school, here at the rink, on Sundays. Figure skating demands a tremendous amount of discipline, and I know she's benefited from that. And she loves doing it. After she gets her gold she'll always have the option of using it professionally. So she's moving forward, even though it does take up a lot of her time, and that's more than many other parents can say about their kids. Both hockey and figure skating are expensive sports, but it's money well spent.

*Some nights later I was eating buffalo wings at Rudolph's when by chance I met Dave Pedersen, who invited me to join his party. Things like that happen in the Midwest. He was in the publishing business and thought my project interesting. He went out of his way to arrange meetings with his friends—those with children—at their homes. That was how I met Leslie, 11, from Bloomington, a suburb of Minneapolis. Leslie was far too prepared for her interview. When I met her she said, "I thought you'd probably ask me what I wanted to do when I grew up, so I've got it down to three possibilities." She went on to speak about the environment, war, hobbies. She had every base covered, determined to impress upon me that she was a focused, capable, and mature young woman. Leslie was typical of a group I would come to call professional kids. I was certain she had been 11 years old for at least 20 years.*

*Leslie was my first pro, and I thought it cute. I also thought it impressive—after all, she really was focused, capable, and mature. But it made my job much more difficult. We sat on the sofa and drank coffee and looked through large, glass doors out at the frosty landscape, and I felt more like a house guest than an interviewer. I was getting nowhere, because Leslie was conducting the interview.*

*Eventually she mentioned, in passing, that a friend of hers had died the year before. I asked if she wouldn't mind talking about it. Her tone changed. She was no longer prepared. She was 11 years old:*

His name was Dennis. He drowned in Lake Minnetonka last year. Nobody really knows what happened. His parents don't even know. His parents were driving the boat—he was kneel-boarding or something like that—and they weren't watching him because they were so close to shore. When they turned and they looked for him, he was gone. They drove around, but they couldn't find him. Then they knew that he had gone under, he had drowned. That night they drag-pulled the lake and they found him.

He was wearing a life vest and everything, but something musta happened to it . . . broke off . . . it wouldn't have mattered though . . . he woulda died anyway, because he broke his neck and his back at the same time. That's the one thing I'm glad for: He died instantly, so he had no pain.

I heard it on the news, which is really bad. Then I was lying in bed and I got a phone call. It was one of my friends telling me that it was him, he was the one who died. It was a real shock. He was a great swimmer. I swam with him a lot.

I was down for, like, a few months. It was hard to believe that he was really dead. It seemed like he just . . . shouldn't have died. It stayed in the back of my head for a long time. We had a counselor at school, and I talked to her and it helped me. She said it was important to think of the good things and the bad things, that you had to try not to think of the bad things. She helped a lot.

I started writing about it, poems and stories, just to try and, like, deal with it. I wrote about our past, all the good things . . . It cheered me up. I wrote a poem called "Way Down Deep":

I will always remember you, Dennis
Way down deep
There will always be a place in my heart
For you
Way down deep
You were a good friend
Why did you have to leave us
I wish you were here
Everyone loves you
Way down deep

*Has it changed you in any way?*

I'm scared of the water. I love swimming; I go in pools all the time. I don't go in lakes. It gives me the same feeling as watching a scary movie. And . . . I know it sounds pretty stupid but, I'm kinda afraid of seaweed. I guess I'm a little more cautious than I was before.

*Have you ever thought about death?*

Yes, I do. I had a dream where Jesus was calling me to take me back to . . . telling me I had to die, and I just screamed. I ran into my mom's room and stayed there. Sometimes I worry about my brother. He dives from too high up at the swimming pool, and he's not that good of a swimmer. I stay in the shallow end.

His family still remembers him. They got an ice boat and they named it after him; they put "Dennis" on the side. I still think about it every now and then. And if I keep thinking about it I get a reaction; I get mad, and I take it out on my brother.

*(She looks through the door at the horizon and speaks with heart-wrenching sincerity.)* The strange thing is, I met Dennis at the lake. We didn't go to the same school or anything, but my family knows some people from over there *(the two lived in neighboring towns)*, and I met Dennis when we were with this other family. We became friends, and we'd meet at the lake and play and swim and stuff. Everything we did had to do with water.

One of the sad things is that there was a drought last year, so I didn't see him as much as usual.

*Well, enough of that. What do you want to be when you grow up?*

*(Smiling)* An architect, a writer, or a teacher.

*Another meeting set up by Dave was with Cheryl, a 13-year-old, in St. Paul. Minneapolis and St. Paul are like Dr. Jekyll and Mr. Hyde. St. Paul is the industrial center, the crime center, home of the generic shopping center. Cheryl's house was on the outskirts—luckily, for her.*

*Cheryl was the best-mannered girl I had ever met, and she made me slightly uneasy, because my manners are less than perfect. She brought me coffee, with a saucer, and set it down quietly on the table. She sat and crossed her legs. Another pro.*

I go to a Montessori school. They started with a woman called Maria Montessori a long time ago. It's different than other schools; I think we really learn more. They teach us more about certain subjects than other schools do. A friend of mine is 15 and goes to public school kitty-corner from mine, and we're learning the same thing in math. We do our homework together.

Right now I have algebra, French, Russian, Latin, literature, chemistry, and history. We have a writing class where we have to debate, verbally. We stand up behind a podium and talk to the class. When you're up there it's you against the class. You debate an issue and the class tries to prove you wrong. You try to get your point across; that's what it's all about. Our school wants you to be independent, not to be scared about talking in front of people, so we do that a lot. We're all used to things like that. Every year some new kids join the school, and they're all nervous about debating, but by the end of the year they're just like us.

I've always been in this school so it's a little hard to compare to anything else. Everything's so different. I've been learning French since I was three. *(The school enrolls children as young as two in a half-day program.)* We work at our own pace—fourth-, fifth- and sixth-graders are all in the same class. You work on your own. There are no grades.

We don't have desks like regular schools do. We don't have to sit in certain places. We just have a round table, and we sit with our friends. That's kinda nice. . . . Yes, things are very close with the teachers. We call them by their first names, and they encourage us to, like, talk to them if we have any problems, even if it has nothing to do with school. I think we have a much closer bond to our teachers than public-school kids do. We can go and ask them for help on a paper or whatever, they know us so well . . .

*(I fumble and spill my coffee. Cheryl says it's all right and goes into the kitchen for paper towels.)*

*When you graduate, how will you be different from other kids?*

Sometimes I think our school might keep us away from reality. It's a very small school. You know everyone. We might be a little sheltered. Gangs and rapes and drugs and a lot of things that are happening in the city, we just don't know anything about. The public-school kids live with it every day. That's about the only thing wrong with the school. I don't know . . . even if we don't know all that's going on, there's a nice, safe feeling at school, and I like that.

We have a very tight community. There are only 42 kids in the junior high. We know everyone personally; we know everything that goes on at home. If you went to a public school with 5,000 people you'd only *really* get to know five or six. The rest are strangers. I don't think I'd like that.

*What about the selection of boys?*

*(Laughs.)* Well, some of the girls complain, because there's only about 20 of them, and they're not the best, but that doesn't bother me. That's why most of the people leave the school—I mean those who do leave. But, the school only goes through eighth grade, so—who really needs that kind of social life in junior high?

*I talked to Cheryl's father after our interview and he told me that, though at first he was skeptical, he thinks he made the right move in sending Cheryl and his older son to Montessori school. "We found out very early that our son was gifted. He was bored in public school. We sent him to the Montessori school, and he was excited about it. He looked forward to going to school."*

# 3

# The Other Side of Town

*By this time a couple of weeks had passed, and I had met some people. I was invited to a Seafood Sunday dinner party in a suburb which is, for good reason, to remain nameless. There was snow and a strong wind when I left there around midnight. The defrost button on my dashboard has long been a cosmetic feature only, and after two or three minutes of driving I couldn't see a thing through the windshield or the rear window. As I was panicking, flashing red lights slid through the icy windows. I had no idea if I was speeding—if I was even on the road.*

*The cop who pulled me over—I'll call him Tom—was riding alone, as cops sometimes do in the suburbs. He made his way to my car, and I folded my hands and rested them on the steering wheel. I learned this gesture from an L.A. cop who said, "When you get pulled over, make sure your hands are visible when he comes to the window. That way he knows you're not reaching for anything. Any cop anywhere'll appreciate that. And it's the best way to get out of a ticket." Tom took my license and came back two minutes later, smiling. It had worked. "You must know some cops," he said. I explained.*

*Tom asked about the clutter in my car (I hadn't bothered to unpack), and I told him what I was doing. He said he had three kids and that he thought the book a great idea.*

*I didn't get a ticket; I didn't get to interview his children. But I did ride with Tom—wedged between a computer and a shotgun—from midnight to six, answering calls, listening to his stories of crime in the Twin Cities, talking about his kids and other kids, and, of course, drinking coffee at the White Castle.*

*Tom was about 35, tall and broad—a real Midwest sportsman. His most remarkable feature was his moustache, which was easily four times wider, longer, and bushier than the average one, and appeared independent of his face—when he moved his head quickly, it really seemed as though face and moustache were only friends.*

*The first call we answered was a report of a suspicious car parked in a shopping center. It* was *suspicious. The car, a Miata, was parked in the very center of an empty parking lot, the motor running. Tom reckoned it was a drug transaction. We came in fast, from behind, skidding to a halt just five feet from the car; Tom turned the spotlight on the back window—all of this causing a general panic inside the Miata. They were two in the car, boy and girl, both 18, both terrified, both naked. Tom followed his moustache back to the patrol car and radioed the story to his colleagues, with provocative embellishment.*

*There wasn't much crime that night. As Tom explained, that was precisely the reason he had moved to the suburbs:*

I grew up in St. Paul and started working on the force there when I got married, about 12 years ago. I watched it get worse and worse. The drug trade caused a lot of problems, a lot of shootings. The gangs came in. One night I was escorting a prisoner, a drug addict, from Minneapolis to a hospital in St. Paul when I got a gun pressed up against the back of my head. It was one of his friends. I was certain they were gonna kill me. That's when I decided to get out. I came here a few years ago.

I mean, the thing is, I was starting a family—I wanted my kids to be safe and to be able to walk to school and everything. Life's much easier out here. Sometimes, on the late shift, there's just nothing to do. I shouldn't tell you this . . . One of the other guys and me got so bored one night last year that we drove out to the railroad tracks and took target practice. We saw some rabbits and we went after 'em, but when we shot the first one we saw it was a jack rabbit—you can't eat them. But that's what it was like. Nice and relaxed.

That's all changing too. It's getting worse out here. The Los Angeles gangs moved into the cities, the Vietnamese gangs are here, drugs are just out of control. The drug dealers come here from the cities to sell drugs to the kids.

There's a new breed of teenager out there. The gangbangers—Crips and Bloods—are carrying machine guns around. They make more money than I do—17-year-olds! They'll kill someone and think nothing of it. They become role models for the younger kids. A 10-year-old kid sees a drug dealer or a gang member with a nice car and jewelry and girls, and that's what he wants to be when he grows up. As a cop you have to readjust; you can't treat them like kids.

You've been talking to the uptown kids. Drive 10 minutes to the other side of Minneapolis and see what those kids have to say. They're living right in the middle of it. I feel sorry for them.

*At about four, Tom called the station to confirm that his supervisor was out. He took me there—the sportsman in him couldn't believe I had never fired a gun. He had in his locker a small collection of handguns, including one of those oversize Clint Eastwood deals. From 4:30 to 5 I stood in the two-man firing range—firing, reloading, firing, reloading—until the floor was littered with scraps of black silhouettes. I could hardly believe I was doing this. I don't like guns. The sensation of power I experienced—that violence at my own hand could be so easily realized—was terrifying. Still, I enjoyed myself wildly. That may not make sense, but there it is.*

*From the Miata to the firing range, Tom had fractured the rule book in several places. He asked that I not use his name nor the name of his town.*

*I contacted the Boys and Girls Club in the section of Minneapolis Tom had spoken of, and went there to talk to the kids. The neighborhood was low-income, predominantly black—the center of drug and gang activity in Minneapolis. The club was a safe haven for neighborhood kids. Still, the neighborhood didn't look* that *bad to me, by New York or Los Angeles standards.*

*The club was full of life. There were kids watching television, shooting pool, playing video games, acting tough, hanging out.*

*When I had talked with the uptown kids, I had often asked, "If you could spend tomorrow with anyone at all, who would it be?" The most common answers were New Kids on the Block, Bart Simpson, and Paula Abdul. I now put the question to James, a stocky 13-year-old, the spitting image of Bo Jackson:*

My dad. My dad's in jail down in Kentucky. My mom and me drive down there every summer to see him. He's gettin' out in five years. He shot somebody, killed 'em. Some girl was messin' with 'im, and he just—it was an accident—he just put out his gun to scare her away, and he pulled the trigger accidentally, 'cause he used to shoot it a lot. He'd shoot like, bottles and stuff. That happened three years ago. He got eight and a half years. I miss him a lot, but it's weird, you know, after three years it's not such a big deal. You just kinda accept it.

He's still my dad—my mom wouldn't never marry anyone else—and we're gettin' back together when he gets out, but . . . last time I was in Kentucky to visit 'im, we couldn't really say nothin'. It's like, "How ya doin'?"

"Fine. How *you* doin'?"

"Fine."

You know what I mean?

Some a my family don't like 'im. They say he's like a murderer and stuff. I don't listen—I know my dad didn't kill 'er on purpose. I know 'e didn't.

*Janette, eight, was the only white girl I talked to at the club. I knew I was in for something the moment I saw her. She was pale and unhealthy looking, and her pasty complexion contrasted dramatically with her dark, somber eyes. She seemed always on the verge of tears, a very troubled, unhappy girl.*

*She never once looked me in the eye during her intense and discursive narrative:*

I want to be a police officer. I think they understand everything—you have to. If you're a police officer and you have somebody who can't hear, then you have to know sign language. You gotta know how to shoot a gun. You gotta know how to use those . . . I don't know what they're called but you gotta know how to use them too. You know what I mean, if somebody doesn't cooperate or they're drunk, if they're drinking or something, then you use these things to make them stop.

I got lost once and I met a police officer named Carl. He was nice. I told him my phone number and he brought me home.

*What were you doing out by yourself?*

Well, I don't know. My mom told me to get out of the house . . . my mom told me to get out of the house, so I got out of the house. She said . . . she said . . . she didn't tell me at what time to be back so, I just wandered off. A dog chased me. That was scary. I thought he was just gonna gobble me up. I walked a long way. . . . Yeah, we had a fight, but I don't remember what it was about. My cat made a mess or something. I get along with my mom. I love her. She's 27. But that's why I want to be a police officer, so I can help people like he helped me, and so I can stop people from drinking.

*Do you know anyone who drinks?*

*(She takes a pen and spins it around on the table. When it stops, she spins it again. During the third spin she answers, eyes glued to the pen.)* My uncles drink. I got three uncles; one's 28, one's 24, and the other is about 30. I got another uncle too, but he doesn't live with us anymore. They like to drink a lot. Larry, Derek and John. John sleeps in the back bedroom and Larry and Derek sleep on the

floor. They drink every day . . . . No, my mom doesn't say anything about it. I told her I didn't like it and she told them that if they didn't stop drinking by April, she'd throw them out of the house. They'll have to go live with my other uncle.

Derek was drinking a lot last night. He drinks till he can't drink any more. Last night he and Larry were playing Up and Down the River. That's a card game where you have to use beer. If you have kings, jacks, aces, you have to drink. I just watch television. I turn it up loud. I turn it up so loud so I can't hear them drinking and screaming and all that other stuff.

John drinks a lot on Fridays. He goes to a blood bank to get money to buy beer. But today he went and he bought groceries with the money. He bought cereal and chips and pop, hot dogs. My mom told him he had to. I like my mom because she brings me here to the club and picks me up later. I like coming here, all the kids.

Last night Derek and Larry had the radio up so loud that I couldn't hear the TV. What I do is, I go and unplug the radio and they say, "What happened to the radio?" They never know what's wrong with it. Or else I take out the batteries and I hide them. Then they're like, "The radio must be broke." They never know. Sometimes Mom tells them that they have to drink in the back room or she'll take all their beer and dump it out in the sink. She gets mad because they buy beer instead of groceries.

Yesterday I taught my mom how to say "happy birthday" in sign language. We learned it in school. Do you want me to teach you?

*I asked one of the counselors about Janette, but no one seemed to know much about her. She was dropped off at the club three or four times a week, and she said little if anything to the other kids. She watched television.*

*Bridgett, 13, was tall and lanky; so tall and lanky that her limbs seemed to shake when she walked, like a dancing skeleton. I could almost hear them crackling.*

*It was obvious she wanted to be somewhere else, and I sensed we wouldn't hit it off. I asked her what the neighborhood was like:*

The biggest problems are drugs, gangs, racism, homelessness, abortion, teenage pregnancy—we got a girl in our school has a two-month baby by a' 18-year-old man and she's only my age, 13. Her mom takes care of the baby when she's in school. Pretty crazy. She told everybody 'bout it. Everybody treats her the same; some girls look up at her 'cause she's got a baby, like she's real mature or somethin'.

If I get pregnant, it would be on me, my problem, 'cause I'm the one who did it. I would have my baby. But I can't say nothin' for other people for the same reason: Everybody's responsible for themself. It's their own choice to have a' abortion. I could never do it, but I believe everyone should have their own choice on that subject.

Most of the girls in my grade, about 70 percent, are sexually, you know . . . Yeah, active. A lot of my friends are sexually active; a lot of 'em is in gangs and stuff. I mean, you can't be surprised that a 13-year-old is havin' sex and all that, when they're hangin' out with the Crips or the Bloods. Some girls have boyfriends that sell drugs . . . I don't know, they get around too fast. There's a corner at my *(junior high)* school where the kids go to smoke pot or whatever.

*(She glares at me, as if I've said something nasty. I have the feeling I've missed something, but I can't imagine what it could be. Suddenly it is apparent that she doesn't like me. She talks down to me.)*

Me and my friends had a problem with this white teacher, and we went to the counselor and principal about it 'cause we thought she was bein' prejudice. She started pickin' on us by tellin' us to get rid of our gum all the time. She hardly never told white kids to throw it out. My friend came to class one day with some a those spandex biker shorts, 'cause it was real hot that day. The teacher wouldn't let us leave the door open, 'cause she said people in the hall would bother us. So my friend asks her if she can open up the windows instead, and the teacher starts goin' crazy—"You're not in charge of this class! Who do you think you are? You shouldn't be wearing those shorts. I won't have you wearing those shorts in my class!" My friend only asked her to open the window 'cause we were all sweatin'!

Then the last straw came. This white girl, Gail, sits next to me in math. One day we took a quiz and we were goin' up to the teacher so she'd correct 'em. Gail goes up and she doesn't even look at her paper and she says, "Very good, Gail," and gives her a' A. I went up and she starts markin' everything wrong, gave me a D. I looked on Gail's paper and we had the same answers. Me and my friends were like, "Hey, they got the same answers, so why you givin' Gail a' A? She asks to see Gail's paper again, and she goes through it checkin' 'em all off and gives her a D too! Gail started cryin', and my friend Marla went up to her and cussed her out, called her a prejudiced bitch.

So we went to the counselor—there's a black woman that works as a counselor—and she talked to us for a' hour when we shoulda been in that teacher's class. *(Laughs.)* The next day we met with the counselor, the principal and the teacher. We told the principal 'bout the time she told me and Marla she wanted to talk to us out in the hall, and when she followed us out she slammed the door in our face, locked it, and went back to teachin' the class. We couldn't get back in. So we told the principal all this and he said, "I see, I see, I see," and we're still in the same class. She acts a little different, but she still picks on us. If we come five minutes late she sends us out; if Becka, this white girl, comes in five minutes late she says, "Sit down and open your book." Everything's still the same, but it's a little different.

*I was happy to be finished with that. Bridgett and her animosity and her dancing bones were irritating. But, if she wasn't sweet or enchanting, she did open up an important subject. Drugs and gangs are the greatest obstacles for today's inner-city kids. I had worked with L.A. gang members on my last book, and I knew the problem well. But I was shocked to find that the L.A. gangs—the Crips and the Bloods—had come as far east as Minneapolis in just a few years. They're heavily armed and vicious as animals, but they execute their violence with businesslike precision. They move into a city, take over the drug trade (often by eliminating the competition), and as Tom indicated, corrupt the local kids. Gang warfare—"gangbanging"—becomes a fact of life.*

*The result: a genocide of inner-city youth. Here's Kevin, 13, who also talked about gangs, and went on to win the award for the most sudden change of subject:*

I wish they could do something about the drugs and the gangs around here. I live over on Chicago and 38th—it's pretty bad from 34th on down. The Crips and the Bloods are causin' lots of problems. A lotta people sell drugs. I was walkin' down the street the other day and some Bloods were hangin' out. They was like, "Hey, Crip," 'cause I was wearin' a blue baseball hat. I was like, "I don't want no trouble. I ain't no Crip."

But that stuff's crazy. You can get killed for wearin' the wrong color hat. Claimin' a set *(declaring yourself a member—the gangs are broken down into smaller, localized "sets")* is real popular. I know a lotta kids want it real bad. They wanna hang with the big-time gangbangers and sell drugs. They wanna be wearin' big gold chains and everythin'.

The new thing around here is to wear L.A. sports clothes. Raider hats and jackets and everything. L.A. Kings stuff. All the gangbangers wear it. I'd like to see those guys get what they deserve. They should take their cars away. I don't like any of that stuff. Most kids do, but not me.

*What makes you different?*

Well, I was hit by a bus. I was riding my bike, and the bus made a left turn and it hit me. I got run over. . . . Yeah, it was his fault. I remember going over the handlebars and seeing the pavement. I was under the bus when I woke up. People were holding my arms down. I went out again, and I came to in the ambulance. They asked me my name. Then I went out again, and when I woke up I was in the intensive-care place with my arms hung up over my head. They told me the bus ran over my arms, a pressure injury; they just exploded. *(He rolls up his shirtsleeves and shows two horrible railroad-track scars running the length of each forearm.)* I got these scars here and one on my leg. I was in intensive care for a week and then in my own room for two more weeks. We're still suing the bus driver. It takes a long time. He paid for all the hospital bills.

*(I wonder if there is any way he can bring this story back to the subject of gangs.)*

I got these scars for the rest of my life—I know what it is to be in the hospital. That's why I won't have nothin' to do with the Crips and the Bloods. If you get in with them, you gonna get hurt, sometime. Someone's always gettin' shot or stabbed. A Crip gets killed, then the Bloods come after the guy who did it, then the Crips go after him . . . None a that stuff's for me. I don't want no more scars.

*Jill, a 16-year-old, was a member of Smart Thinking, a club-within-the-club teaching younger kids to do the right thing. She was sharp, and she had the charming habit of grabbing my wrist whenever she made an important point, or whenever she agreed with or found funny something I said. A gifted speaker, Jill varied her pace and pitch like an anchorwoman:*

People think the Midwest is all corn and tractors and everything, but it's not. Not here. The Twin Cities have nothing to do with the Midwest. An hour south of here it's like people think, but not here. It's a strange thing being a black person in Minnesota. In the Twin Cities you're pretty comfortable, but anywhere else . . . I mean, for me, Minneapolis *is* Minnesota. I went to Duluth one time and I only saw one other black person the whole time I was there, and he was cleaning the floor.

The drug situation in Minneapolis and St. Paul is pretty much out of control, or on its way. You can buy anything you want anytime. Crack is the biggest drug. So many people are dealin'. They buy gold earrings for their girlfriends, and they wear their beepers to school. They put a ban on beepers and they restricted jewelry—the one thing I don't like is that now you can't wear five-finger rings, or even two-finger rings, because they say they're like brass knuckles. The principals are tightening up on it. They know who the drug dealers and the gangbangers are.

The gang problem is getting really bad. Some people came out from Los Angeles to branch out their gangs, the Crips and the Bloods. They set up here and get people here all into it, and they start selling drugs. Then they start fighting with the local gangs. They're starting to move into the suburbs. *(She smiles. She's just loving the whole thing, the opportunity to express herself.)*

In my grade, I'd say 85, 90 percent of the girls are having sex. This year we have 26 pregnant girls, because we have this program where there's day care and everything. They have to take these one-hour parenting courses every day, in addition to their regular classes. Some of them are my friends. They just didn't want to have abortions. They don't believe in it—I think it depends on how much you got going for you. There's a guy at school who got his girlfriend pregnant, and he had a lot going for him, basketball scholarship, and he wasn't ready for something like that, so he wanted her to get an abortion. There are girls who don't want an abortion just because they want to trap the guy. I think everyone has to make their own choice.

Race problems are getting worse . . . black, white, Vietnamese. People think like, "Minnesota . . . the north . . . people aren't like that," but there's a lot of tension.

At the beginning of this school year, there was a lot of times where blacks were getting beat up by whites or the other way around. No reason. People don't want to talk about it, but I see it every day. My school's not so bad because it's predominantly black, but two others, Edison and Southwest, they've got *big* problems. It was in the news and everything.

*Every time I've been out I've seen 10 interracial couples. I've seen more here in one week than I did in six months in Los Angeles. Always a black guy with a white girl.*

Yeah, isn't that strange? *(She laughs and grabs my wrist.)* It doesn't really back up what I've been saying, does it. Yeah, that's true, it's real popular, and it's a big problem between black girls and white girls, and black girls and black guys. No, white guys don't figure into it, so you can just relax. *(Laughs.)* A lotta my friends are like, "No, no, I'd never go out with a white dude," and they get really mad when a black guy will go out with a white girl. I used to be like that. It happens because—I know as a black girl that I want to be in control. Black women are like that, and that's why there are so many interracial couples. Every time you see one you'll notice that the white girl does everything the black guy tells her to do. She submits herself to him. A black woman would just say, "Uh-uh, I ain't doin' that." *(Laughs.)* At school, most of the guys who go out with white girls try to deny it, like, "I'm just doin' it for the sex." There are also some guys who do it to get back at their girlfriends. It's never really sincere at the high-school level.

If I took a survey, I know that at least 50 percent of the black guys in my school have been with a white girl. Most of them will never admit it because, like, in my school, after a black guy goes out with a white girl he's through. Black women won't talk to him. He'll stay with the white girl for the rest of his life.

The whole thing's so strange. Some people tell me I talk white, I act white. I've noticed that when a white girl starts going out with a black guy she becomes like, the Queen of Rap, gold chains and everything. I don't have so many white friends because of that.

I know one girl who goes out with a white guy, but they both keep it seriously locked up in the closet. They're a real minority. *(Laughs.)* They really love each other.

*Thank God for sports. No matter what the neighborhood, sports are the universal form of escape. For kids, especially ghetto kids, sports stars are gods—except, of course, those serving time for rape, drug possession or murder. Minneapolis was described in athletic terms by Danny, a 13-year-old wearing a baseball cap, a football shirt, and basketball shoes:*

The best thing about the Twin Cities is the Timberwolves. We got Pooh Richardson. I'd like to play for them someday. I've been to four of their games. They almost beat the Lakers last week. Man, that Pooh Richardson's got it all. He's so *smoooooth.* Sometimes I think about what it would be like to be him.

I go to Vikings games, Northstars, I go to see the University of Minnesota Gophers a lot. I like going to see the Twins over at the Metrodome.

*Who's got the best chow of all the stadiums?*

The Metrodome has the best dogs, but their pop runs kinda high. But you get a souvenir cup with the $2.35 pop with all the teams on it. The Gophers play at Williams Arena, but there isn't much to eat over there. The Northstars play at the Met Center—they've got those nachos. You get your choice if you want peppers. The Metrodome has the best food. They got people coming around selling licorice and everything. You don't ever have to get up. Man, I wish I had enough money to just live in those places all the time.

*And then there was Teddy Johnson, 10, the Hugh Hefner–Michael Jordan of East Minneapolis. Everything about him was smooth: smooth clothes, smooth voice, smooth speech, smooth name, the classic smooth gait of a ladies' man. Teddy was one of my very favorites:*

School's OK. I got this teacher—she doesn't like work. You never see her doin' work; she's just sittin' there suckin' on candy and stuff like that. It's not like math, where you gotta work. She even gives *us* candy and cookies when we do our silent reading. Man, we never do anything in her class.

The best thing about school's that I like a whole bunch of sixth graders—and they're big and tall and everything. I like some of the fifth graders too. There's one who's short for a fifth grader; I like her a lot and she likes me too. She's a grade ahead of me, so we write notes and pass 'em through the classes. She's on my bus. She comes here to the club and she sees me lookin' at other girls. She says, "Don't be lookin' at other girls. You're supposed to be lookin' at me." And if I keep on lookin' at 'em, she turns around and slaps me. It hurts. *(He rubs his cheek.)* Then I say I'm sorry.

I don't like the girls in my own grade. They're too ugly—*Yeah*! One girl—I like her too, I go with her too. Her name is Caren. Oh man . . . she looks better than anybody. I got put in the back of the classroom for not listenin' and she came back to me. I says, "Watcha doin' back here?" and she says, "It's boring up there." She asked me who I liked and I told her I didn't know. She gets real serious, like, "Who do you like?" "I don't know." She says, "Well, I like someone and his name ends with y." I said, "Denny." She said no. I said, "Dusty." She said no. Those were the only ones I could think of. So I says, "Me?" And she says yes. I told her, "I like you too." Her cheeks got all red and redder.

*Did you feel like the heavyweight champion of the world?*

Yes. She kinda scooted over next to me too. And I put my arm around her.

*Have you always been so popular with the girls?*

No, I used to be like everyone else, but then I got my hair cut, and curled too. It's startin' to grow back like a bush. I gotta get it cut again. *(His bushiest hair is no more than half an inch long. The sides are cut to the scalp.)* I always keep the sides like this, like Pooh Richardson. I had me a Mike Tyson flat-top too. But everyone liked this haircut when I first got it. Even the teachers liked it—we have one teacher—she's so nice. She's real pretty. Her name's Miss Lawrence. I give her a note every day. It's not easy to work in her class. Man, I wish I was in the sixth grade.

*What's the difference between a sixth-grade girl and a fourth grader?*

There's a big difference. You can tell the sixth graders because they're always talkin' and they're snappin,' and sometimes I think, "Man, I wish I was a sixth grader." They don't like younger kids. They don't mess with me—I got bodyguards at the school. Nobody picks on me 'cause they know what'll be wrong with them. You see, I play a lot of basketball, 'cause that's my favorite sport, and my whole school knows that. I play with the sixth graders, and I'm the best out there. So if they want to be my bodyguard or they want my autograph, that's OK. . . . Yes, the girls ask for my autograph 'cause they think I'm gonna be a famous basketball player. That's what makes me popular. I got pretty good at writin' my name. That's why older girls wanna go out with me.

It's a good thing I got those bodyguards too, 'cause it gets pretty rough out there—lotta fights and stuff. They know what'll happen if they mess with me.

*What makes you different than other kids your age?*

I look better than them, I talk better, I play better basketball, I'm cleaner than them, I got better clothes than they do, I got better shoes—I just got a pair of Air Jordans.

*Do you have any problems at all?*

Well, I don't like it when ugly girls ask me for my autograph.

*Teddy was my last interview. I talked to the club director for a while, packed up, and made for the door. I passed the television room on my way out. Teddy Johnson was watching college basketball. He was being mobbed by "babes"—at least 10 girls surrounded him. There was not another boy in sight. He smiled to me and waved good-bye.*

*I was encouraged by these first interviews. I got along well with all the kids and the conversation flowed. I saw that kids would often drop hints or cite obscure references to segue into certain issues that were bothering them. Some were intimidated by the tape recorder, but that was to be expected. With each successive child and teenager I felt more at home—fluent with their language, better able to read their faces and understand the tone of their voices.*

# 4

# The Mississippi Valley

*I left Minneapolis on April 16 in a blizzard. Dave Pedersen had put me in touch with Dan Block, an old friend of his who lived in Houston, Minnesota, a tiny town in the southeastern corner of the state, close to the vertex of the Iowa border and the Mississippi River. Dan and his wife invited me to spend the night there to see what life was like for kids in the middle of nowhere. I was anxious to learn the advantages and disadvantages of small-town living, as they appear to the kids themselves.*

*Once in town I was fetched by Dan and guided through the labyrinth of dirt and gravel roads leading to his home. It is beautiful and diverse country, grassy and mountainous, but the weather that day made everything drab. The snow turned to drizzle and the dirt roads turned swampy; when we arrived at the house my car was a mud pie. As a matter of fact, my car remained a muddy eyesore until I hosed it down outside the Elvis Presley Boulevard Inn and Lounge in Memphis, in the afternoon heat, one week later.*

*The Block home—built by Dan himself—was buzzing with activity. Five kids, most of them white-haired, collided in the hallway at short intervals, making the most of their Easter vacation. I spoke with them, walked around, and looked at the photographs on the knickknack shelves. Upstairs, I put my shoe in a bowl filled with something akin to bean curd. It had been invented and abandoned by the youngest girl, a four-year-old. Downstairs, a nine-year-old trumpet-playing Block was struggling through "Heart and Soul." The second-oldest girl was busy trying to expose the film in my camera. The Block home was swinging.*

*Before dinner I talked with Rachel, 14, the oldest. She was wrapped in olive-drab army wear, a mod look I didn't expect to find in Houston.*

*I could sense that Rachel was looking forward to our talk. The product of involved, creative, and open-minded parents, she was articulate and eager to communicate. She attacked Houston with alacrity:*

I guess it's pretty boring to live out here in the middle of nowhere. Nobody thinks so—"Oh, you're *soooo* lucky to live down there. You get to go on walks and everything!" I never go on walks. City people like it here for about two days, then they're ready to kill themselves.

There's not much to do—about the only thing there is to do is get in trouble, so that's mostly what we do. *(Laughs.)* Like our neighbors, the older kids, they have parties all the time. There's always a party somewhere. Don't walk on the roads around here at night. *(Laughs.)*

A lot of the people here, their families have a long history in Houston. I think they're all pretty happy here—a lot of my friends are happy here—but I'm not happy here. I guess I take a lot of the country life-style for granted—the air, the space—I'd probably miss it if I was gone for a long time. But I won't let that hold me back. I'm ready to leave at any time. *(Laughs.)*

It's so isolated! There's about 200 kids in our school—that's seventh through twelfth grade. You know everybody. Everybody knows everything about you—they know things about you that *you* don't even know. I live seven miles from town—and the town is isolated itself. There's two banks, a liquor store, a gas station—that's pretty much Main Street. We've got Albert the cop, who just sits in his car all the time and doesn't even put his radar on. But anyway, someone wants to come to the house and it's like, impossible: "Well, you take this dirt road a couple miles to the gravel road and you follow that to another dirt road . . ." Would you have found this place if my dad hadn't come to get you? *(No, I wouldn't have. And I got lost on the way out.)* You read stories about people who come from towns with a thousand people, and they're all sheltered and everything. I don't want to be like that.

In a town like this, you can't really do anything different without everyone saying you're strange. They say that about me 'cause I'm a vegetarian and this and that. There was a boy in school who, out of nowhere, got a mohawk. I loved it because it was different. I couldn't believe he did it. The public reaction was like, "What the hell did you do to your hair?" He grew it out and that was the end of it.

I don't really fit in with the rest of the people. I dress differently and everything. Hunting is big sport here; it's a hunting town. I'm a vegetarian. I think about life outside of Houston. Like, they serve tuna for lunch at school, and I was trying to get them to stop, and then trying to get the kids to stop before they got in the lunch line, because of all the dolphins tuna fishermen kill. They were like, "If just a few people don't eat tuna it's not gonna change anything." I went to the principal and asked him to stop buying the tuna. *(In a deep voice)* "Well, would you stop eating meat because of all the ants that cows step on in the fields?" *Oooo,* I hate that attitude. It's just typical of Houston.

*(She's on a roll, letting it all out excitedly. She moves to the alcove of her bedroom, sits atop a storage chest, pulls her knees to her chin and releases a deep breath, putting on the brakes. She chuckles at her enthusiasm and continues at a slower pace.)*

It's a pretty old-fashioned town, maybe a little chauvinistic. We're all Lutherans, but not too serious about it—it's the morality part of religion that comes through. We have a Bible instruction class, and I got into a tiny argument with my pastor last week. He was talking about concubines, and how a man having a concubine isn't a sin. I said it was adultery, and he was like, "Naw, they live like they're married." There's a lot of double standards like that. I don't think men *have* to be the leaders of the households even if the Bible says they should.

*How did you end up such a free thinker?*

*(She smiles again and checks her renewed excitement.)* I don't know. Not liking where I'm growing up. The strange thing is that I'm all alone; I'm the only kid who feels that way. I guess a lot of it comes from my parents; they always did things their own way. In the '70s my parents were the classic long-haired rebel hippies, believe it or not. *(Laughs.)* Both my mom and dad grew up in Minneapolis and went to the University of Minnesota. They decided they wanted to live somewhere else. My mom said, "How about Arizona?" So they moved to Arizona. So they were there for one week and they decided they hated it, so they came straight back. They were driving the scenic route, and that took them right through Houston. They loved the area, so they went to the first realty office and bought this land. They came back and forth from the cities every weekend and worked on the house—they lived in tents. Eventually they moved down here for good.

Everything you see here on our property was built by my dad: the house, the shed . . . We've got 160 acres, dogs, cats, horses . . . My mom is real big on gardening. She grows everything, and when she's not doing that she's talking about gardening. Together they made all of this.

*Where are you going to raise your own kids?*

I want them to be in the middle—not in the city, not in the sticks. I think things are changing; the cities move too fast, and the small towns like this are losing their charm, the whole peaceful, beautiful thing. I'll probably live in the suburbs.

Education's another thing. I don't think the education is that great in towns like this. We don't get a foreign language until ninth grade, and that's only one, Spanish. And that's an elective. I'd like to take Russian, or French. I mean, I hope I can handle the shock of going to college after being here, in a class of 38.

I guess I'm being a little one-sided. I'm sure I'm more independent than big-city kids. I'm just ready to get out. I go to visit my grandmother every now and then in Minneapolis. I go shopping, walk around . . . It's just better. It's louder, there's more people, so much to do. It's a strange feeling, that all these people are walking by you and you don't know any of them. When you walk down the street in Houston, you know everybody. You have to wave to them all.

*Rachel was the only child old enough to be restless—and restlessness is natural enough among teens; any teenager, from the big cities to the wilderness, eventually feels the urge to be somewhere else. Still, I felt she was fond of and attached to her surroundings. I even caught her in the backyard, at sundown, taking in the scenery.*

*I sat with the six-year-old Block girl for 30 minutes, during which time she did nothing other than present for me, piece by piece, her entire wardrobe, pausing occasionally to relate the history of a particular piece: how it came to be hers, functions where it was worn . . .*

*The other kids left me a solid impression of one way in which small-town children differ, in general, from their big-city counterparts: They are more imaginative and less worldly. Their lives are more refined, absent of city chaos and clutter. The Block house had one television, which received only two channels. Without the imposition of MTV and video arcades, and without the opportunity to hang out in shopping-mall pizza places, the rural kids I met seemed forced to* think *and* feel. *They developed their own impressions; they invented their own games; they exercised their minds, and their senses bloomed. They were left to be children. For the Block kids, any turn of a corner, any tree in the yard, could be the beginning of a new adventure. Family problems, problems of the world, are absorbed, as they should be, by the whimsicality and innocence of youth. City kids I met were right in the middle of it. They were products of ad campaigns, trends, peer pressure, and all the bustle of a big city, so they were more uniform. If not imaginative they were streetwise, more worldly.*

*A couple of the Blocks' friends came over, and there was a big dinner. We sat at the table for two hours and I enjoyed myself hugely. The next day I started south on 61, which hugs the Mississippi all the way down to Baton Rouge.*

*Iowa is one of those places where, when you turn on the radio, there's still the danger of hearing "Seasons in the Sun" by Terry Jacks. As I drove, passing one flat, yawning field after another, I had the feeling someone was holding my back wheels off the ground. Time moves slowly in Iowa. The state's blank landscape and retroactive radio made it impossible to drive for long, so I stopped at a truck-stop diner by Davenport and experienced one of the great midwestern specialties: chicken-fried steak, with mounds of mashed potatoes and gravy. By this time I had adopted a truck-stop diet so perverse and unhealthy that I'm certain it would have killed a lesser man. I still don't know exactly what a chicken-fried steak is, but I recommend it.*

*This meal, like every other meal I had in roadside diners throughout the country, was served to me by Dolly, a stout, 50-year-old woman with rhinestone glasses clipped to her cardigan.*

*The best thing about truck stops is that it's easy to meet people, or at least to join the general conversation. In the booth next to mine sat a couple and their son. I asked if they knew an interesting route that would bring me closer to Florida, my next major stop. We talked for a while. The Braddocks were in the construction business in and around Peoria, Illinois. They were on their way from an Easter family gathering in Iowa. I told them what I was doing—by this time I had an official letter of introduction from my publisher—and 75 miles later I was in Peoria with an invitation to spend the night in the guest room. I could hardly believe my luck.*

*Brian was 13 years old. He went to school, skateboarded, and mowed the lawn on Sundays. He was very tall for his age, and devotion to daily workouts had already yielded him a powerful build.*

*He had an older brother, in his freshman year at college, whom he spoke about at length:*

My brother's like, the family success story. He got straight *A*'s all through school; he won all these prizes and stuff. He got a scholarship to the University of Chicago for science.

I'm not as smart as him—I never will be. And I don't like science. And it sucks because my parents want me to be as successful as him. But I don't get *A*'s, I get *B*'s or *C*'s. My teachers are always comparing me to him, you know, 'cause they all know him.

*That must be irritating.*

It is! It really pisses me off. I'm just tryin' to be myself. Sometimes I wanna tell my pop, like, "Hey, you do construction stuff. You're not a surgeon or a scientist—why should I have to be?"

I'm a really good baseball player. I wanna play professional baseball—maybe I could get a scholarship for that, an athletic scholarship. And even if I don't, anything's better than going to college for 50 years looking into microscopes all day long. I mean, what's the point? He never had any fun—he just works all the time. He never had a girlfriend. I don't wanna be like that. I'd rather fix roofs.

My pop talks about having goals and stuff, working at something until you get it. I understand it—he says I don't.

I'm popular at school. Everyone knows who I am and I'm only in seventh grade. And that's because I play baseball and I work real hard at it—hard enough to be one of the best. In school, if you don't, like, excel in something then you're a nobody. I do excel in baseball so I'm a somebody. And that's like being successful.

*How did your brother and you get along when he was living here?*

Well, he's always studyin' or something, and I'm always outside . . . He was always playin' Mr. Serious, you know what I mean? He talks to you like he's a lawyer or somethin'. He's real into it, real into being smart. All my friends always call him Alex, 'cause of Alex on "Family Ties." Then I say, "Yeah, but the difference is Alex has a girlfriend. A real cute one too."

*(Brian is brimming with bitterness and spite and fury. I imagine him muscling his classmates into coughing up their lunch money.)*

We got in a fight last year—I can't even remember what it was about. He pushed me and I went and tried to punch 'im, but that wasn't easy 'cause he's a lot taller than me. But I got the best of it. If my father didn't break it up I probably woulda beat 'im. I was 12 and he was 17.

*Are you jealous of him at all?*

No way! I mean, I don't want what he's got. Like I said, I don't wanna be no rocket scientist. I know he's gonna be real rich, but that doesn't bother me. My pop loves that—he says that my brother'll be making forty thousand in his first year out of college. But I'd rather be me than him. The only thing that bothers me is that everybody thinks that he's better just because he's gonna be a scientist or whatever. If I make it to the pros, doesn't that make me just as good as him? Doesn't that take just as much work? It takes more! But people think being a real brain like that is the greatest thing in the world.

I'm not a brain, but I'd like to see how he'd do in *my* world. That would be fun. I know it's pretty stupid and everything, but sometimes I daydream that I'm pitching a ball game and my brother's the batter; it's the bottom of the ninth, two outs, full count, and it's me and him . . .

*An angry boy. Not one of my favorites, either. I was surprised that he offered these comments of his own accord—I didn't ask him about his brother—and I was also surprised by the nasty and frenetic way he issued them. It was a release for him. He used our interview the same way an overwrought businessman sucks a happy-hour cocktail, to put the day behind him. Several kids I met later used their interviews to the same end.*

*I got lost getting back to Route 61, and it was already three the next afternoon when I reached Hannibal, Missouri, where I lost my way again. Somewhere south of Hannibal I stopped in a one-street town, 20 miles or so from the highway. I parked in front of a run-down café, next to a Rexall pharmacy, and went in for lunch, hoping luck was still with me.*

*Once on the other side of the frayed screen door I knew luck, at best, would get me back out. The moment I walked in everything stopped: People stopped talking and stared at me. The two enormous women in the open kitchen paused over their pork snouts. In my imagination the music stopped as well. I took the only available table and tried to hide my camera under my coat.*

*No one came to take my order so I went to the kitchen and asked for a ham sandwich. The woman nodded. Ten minutes later she brought it and nodded again. She said not a single word. Now, the plaid shirt sitting next to me was also eating a ham sandwich—it was the daily special. His had french fries, mine didn't; his had a lettuce-and-tomato garnish, mine didn't; his was stuffed with ham and cheese, mine had a single slice of each. I ate, paid, and made for the door. The plaid shirt, looking down at his plate, said, "Now you have yusself a nass day." Going back to my car, I saw myself in the town park, an apple in my mouth, slowly rotating over a spit while the children fought for basting dibs.*

*Sitting in the car I heard a commotion. Down the street, a black woman was having it out with a black man. Some people on the sidewalk stopped to watch after she slapped him a single time. Just as the incident ended, four policemen materialized, handcuffed the man and woman, then handcuffed all the black passersby on the sidewalk and threw them against a fence, telling them to sit down and shut up. I'll never forget that day—it was like going back in time.*

*I drove to St. Louis to see the arch and the steamboats. Motel 6, eggs Benedict, java, 200 miles to Memphis, Tennessee.*

*I was having no luck finding kids to talk to, so I decided to stay in Memphis a couple of days and make a concentrated effort. I picked Memphis because of Graceland—I wanted to see the King's home, if not the King himself. I took the tour the same afternoon I arrived. There were Japanese and Europeans on the tour, but most interesting were the locals—Tennessee folk—who I suppose were making a sort of annual pilgrimage.*

*The girl who guided us was 16, a tiny blond southern belle. I talked to her while the others were examining Elvis's handguns.*

*"How much does Elvis really mean to Memphis?"*

*"Well, Elvis is the Kang. Memphis was 'is favorite place in the whole world—that's why he built Graceland heah. Elvis's a paht of this town. It's history. That's why I like this job so much; there can't be more'n 50 people alive who've toured people 'round Graceland."*

*I spent a half hour in the Graceland gift shop and mailed some Elvis thimbles and Elvis collapsible drinking cups to friends from the adjoining Graceland Post Office.*

*Back in the parking lot I watched a group of pilgrims on the the way to their truck: a husband, wife, baby, and a boy of about 10. The father—this is true—wore dyed black hair, a white leather jumpsuit with rhinestones, and six-inch sideburns. He was Elvis.*

*I tried to imagine interviewing a 10-year-old boy whose dad thought he was Elvis, but it was not to be.*

*The only kid I interviewed in Memphis was Jerry, 12, whose parents I met by chance. The family owned a mortuary, where they also lived. They were nice people. Like many other people I met in the South, they had no southern accent. At their request, I won't say anything more about the family or their business:*

*Jerry, what's it like to live in a mortuary?*

Well, the kids in school tease me sometimes. They call me a grave digger and stuff like that. It doesn't really bother me. I mean, I wouldn't wanna live in a graveyard or nothin', but this is just like a normal house, except when there's someone, you know, downstairs. When they're having a service I just stay upstairs until it's over.

*Do you ever get tired of seeing so much death?*

Like my dad says, dyin's a part of life. Everyone's gonna die. When you're 80 or 90, *you* know you're gonna die—you have to expect it. That's why, when we have an old person, everything's pretty calm. People cry, but it's not too bad. That's the thing I don't like about bein' here, is when they cry a lot. It's really bad when it's not an old person that died. If it's a kid the people go nuts, the family and stuff. There was a boy my age got hit by a truck—the driver was drunk or somethin'—and his mother was screamin' and howlin'. That was bad—it's always bad when it's an accident, some kinda surprise—kids aren't supposed to die. Those things are tough on my father too, 'cause they're messy. The bodies need a lot of work to make them look normal again, if they've been dragged by a truck. Dad says a lot more kids die now than when he was young; it's more dangerous out there now—he doesn't like workin' on young people.

There was a kid about 17 got murdered by accident—they thought he was messin' up a drug deal or somethin'. All the kids' friends from school and all his family from all over Tennessee passed through this place. Everyone was screamin'. That one was the worst. After that I was thinkin', "God, I hope that never happens to me." It's weird to think you can die so easily. You can just walk across the street and get run over. You can walk down the street and someone thinks you're someone else and blows your head off. Anything can happen anytime. But I'm better off from livin' in a mortuary; I'm used to it. If someone I know dies it wouldn't freak me out like most other kids. I'm used to seein' dead people. No sir, I'm not scared of dyin'. I just don't think it could happen to me soon, with my dad bein' a mortician and all. It's too stupid to have your own dad work on you and clean you up and everything.

*Do you want to be a mortician?*

No, I don't think so. I wanna try something different, and besides, too many people die, there's too much work. *(Laughs.)* That's what my dad says. But I like what my dad does. I think it's really important. He makes them look calm and normal, and that helps out the families. When he gets a body that's in real bad shape, he works hard to make it look good; then it's easier for the mother and father.

*I liked Memphis and I found the people there friendly. They like to enjoy themselves, and it seemed as if they didn't let much worry them—a trait I always admire.*

*I drifted around Mississippi until I became hopelessly lost. I expected to find the same southern wariness of strangers I had found in Missouri, so I was surprised when, outside a convenience store, 10 people gathered around me to offer directions. But the directions led nowhere. I made four or five concentric circles and then gave up hope. A word about directions: All through my trip people stopped whatever they were doing to give me bad directions. They rarely got me where I wanted to go. Was I being duped, or do people know so little about their own neighborhoods?*

*Somehow I ended up in Montgomery, Alabama. Ten miles outside of town I stopped for gas at a service station from the '50s—the kind with the tubular gas pumps. While an old man in overalls filled the tank I asked for directions to the downtown area. The reply: "Boy, what in the hell do you wanna go to Montgomery for?" I laughed—I thought he was joking. He wasn't. Later I was told that my arrival in the town coincided with some racial disturbance, or perhaps the anniversary of some racial disturbance.*

*The town was deserted and unreal, a plastic model in a corked bottle. The windows of clothing stores displayed polyester slacks and wide-collared shirts. The few people on the streets looked at their shoes as they walked. It brought me right back to the café in Missouri. I have never been in such a dismal, unwelcoming place.*

*The next morning I left Montgomery depressed and arrived in Tallahassee feeling worse. Super 8, eggs Benedict, java. Fifteen hundred miles from Minneapolis to Tallahassee and I had interviewed three kids. I had tried to talk to several others, but their parents wouldn't allow it.*

*Luckily, I had access to an apartment in Delray Beach, 20 miles south of West Palm Beach, home of the early-bird special, and had already arranged for several interviews. Starting early in the morning I drove the Florida Turnpike to I-95, traveling through sweet-smelling citrus fields and unbearable heat (my car's air conditioning worked as well as the defrost), and arrived in Delray Beach after seven hours. Once out of the car, I saw that the left side of my body was viciously burned by the sun. A trucker's sunburn.*

*That was April 26. Ten days earlier I had left Minneapolis in a blizzard. If America's cities and children are becoming more uniform, the climate is as diverse as ever.*

# 5

# Delray Beach, Florida

*There are some things everyone knows about Florida—South Florida anyway: It's hot; it's peopled with retirees, the elderly, and transients; it holds a prominent position in the world drug trade. Florida conjures the image of palm trees, golf courses, beach vacations, neon colors, corrupt policemen, Cuban drug dealers, and, of course, "spring breakers" with beer-dispensing hats that allow the wearer to suck Budweiser without actually holding the can. All in all an extraordinary image. But how does it influence growing minds?*

*I had spent several spring breaks in Florida when I was in high school, and the place, for me, always represented a kind of lawlessness. I always thought, "School's out, this is Florida, I can do whatever I want." My father caught me once, wildly drunk, when I was 16 or so. My excuse: "Yeah but, this is Florida Dad." Curiously enough he bought it.*

*Most of the kids I talked to here were transients who preferred "home" to lawless Florida ("It's a nice place to visit but . . ."). "*The Hell That Is Florida*" was the overwhelming topic of choice in our talks. I interviewed a very clever 16-year-old in Fort Lauderdale who did a nice job of summarizing his Florida experience:*

I was born in Summit, New Jersey, but I've lived here for six years. Wow, I really hate this place. I mean, how long can you swim and drink before you wanna do something else? That's all there is. You can grow up to be a golf pro or a crack dealer. This place is like the twilight zone.

I like it better up north; there are lotsa young people. This is just a tourist trap. I don't have one friend that was born here. Everybody's from New Jersey. Everyone comes here when they don't know what else to do.

*The few natives I met spoke of little but the ongoing invasion. One of them was Cindy, 14:*

I'm a native Delrayer; I live in the old historical area. When we first moved here, there was nothing but pineapple fields and stuff. We're a dying species, the dying Floridians.

I work at an air-conditioning agency. You can't win, summer or winter. The old people—in the winter we'll get a cold snap, *(sarcastically)* all the way down to 50 degrees—the old people turn on their heat and it doesn't work. They call up and expect you to be there in five minutes. They have no consideration for anyone but themselves. You have to have air conditioning here in the summer—the old people will die without it. Hundreds of people call up for repairs, I take the calls, but these old New Yorkers insist that we come to them first. You can't get them off the phone. They scream at me. Every one of them demands to talk to my boss, then the president, the owner . . . then they call back in an hour, talk to someone else and say that I promised someone would be there two hours ago to fix the AC—they're like little babies sometimes. I don't know, you learn not to let it get to you.

It's like we lost our home. My family used to know everyone else who lived in Delray—it was small. Now it's filled with rich old people and college kids who treat us like shit—like they can just come here and do whatever they want.

*The following interviews were conducted at Atlantic High School in Delray Beach. The student body was an unlikely blend of rich white kids from the North, lower-middle-class white locals, and black kids from the*

*Delray ghetto, a dilapidated danger zone remarkably situated between the wealthy beachfront and inland retirement communities.*

*Atlantic is not a school where kids come to learn, but an air-conditioned place where they meet to plan the coming weekend. The teachers I met were all very devoted and deserving of praise, if not for the honor students they produce, then for the dedication it takes to wear a jacket and tie in 95-degree heat. I suppose the problem is lawlessness. In a place like South Florida, what do you need smarts for? According to Nat, 15, it takes legislation just to keep kids in school:*

Florida has a new law where you can't have 10 unexcused absences from school without losing your driver's license. If you drop out, the same thing happens; you have to be in school to get your license. I think that's great. I'm sure enrollment is up. Either that or there's a lot of kids driving without a license.

Most of the kids here don't get anything out of school. They just come to hang around or talk to their girlfriends or make money if they sell marijuana.

*The girls at Atlantic had long blond hair, dark eyebrows, two dollars' worth of blusher and tight blue jeans. It was my impression that the kids at Atlantic (with the exception of the exceptional kids, most of whom were sent to talk to me) were boorish and propelled by the most basic instincts. They lacked ambition and verve; they fit the stereotype of shiftless adults on welfare.*

*Wendy, 14, was a cute girl. Fluffy blond hair covered her narrow shoulders, and big, beautiful, chocolate-brown deer eyes gave her a look of vulnerability always popular at the high-school level. She spoke of her social life and of relationships in general:*

I don't get along with my father. My parents aren't divorced or separated or anything; I just don't talk to my dad very much. My mom tells me what I can or can't do; my dad doesn't have anything to do with it. I guess that's a little strange. They were separated for a while a couple of years ago, and *then* I spent a lot of time with him, you know: I'd go to stay with him part of the time. I can remember thinking it'd be nice if they got divorced so I could keep spending time with him. But, they got back together. *(Laughs.)* Now, when I get home and my dad's there, it's like, "Hey Dad."

"Hi."

"I'm goin' to watch a baseball game."

"OK, bye."

Then I go to bed when I get home, so I don't ever really talk to him all day.

I'm real close to my mom. I can tell her just about anything—except boy stuff; I talk to my older sister about that. If I do anything wrong I've gotta deal with my father. My mom always threatens me with it—"If you do this you're gonna have to go to Dad." I try not to do anything wrong. I guess it's normal for relationships not to work. All my friends' parents are divorced. My sister got married four months ago, and they just had a big fight—all simple problems they could solve if they tried to work it out, but she's being stubborn; she's saying she wants a divorce. I bet a lot of these things could be worked out if the people just worked on it a little bit.

I mean, my sister's from my mom's first marriage. My mom's first husband—they still talk—he's been married two times since then. She left him 'cause he was an alcoholic. The crazy thing is, like, that's normal.

*As our conversation continued, I discovered that Wendy was always ready to launch into a self-deprecating story. Her vulnerability was not just a look; emotionally she was defenseless, and could be easily duped or taken advantage of. In the soap-opera world of high-school relations, Wendy was a walking bull's-eye.*

There's this guy Steve I liked a lot, but he's got a girlfriend. I started to like him a lot—he's a junior. His friend Dave is a good friend of mine, so we all went out one night to Bass Creek—that's where everyone goes to hang out and drink or whatever. I brought along a girlfriend of mine, and of course, Steve ended up takin' her for a walk and messin' around with her. He didn't know I liked him. The next day he told her he had a girlfriend and stuff.

About three weeks later a bunch of us went to the movies. Steve was there without his girlfriend. And some stuff happened.

And then . . . he's a jerk. *(Laughs.)* He is. I knew he had a girlfriend but I decided to just forget about it. I started seein' him more and more; he'd come over my house all the time. Over spring break we spent a lot of time at my girlfriend's house, because she lives right between me and Steve. Her mom found out that he had a girlfriend one day when he was there and she flipped out. She slapped him! She said, "You're scum and slime! You need to decide who you want to be with."

*Is this lady divorced?*

Yup. *(Laughs.)* Probably wasn't the first time she said those things to a man. But anyway, Steve just laughed at it. He didn't care. I saw him in the library today, and he was like, "I never get to see you anymore." He's a jerk. He asked me to go out with him tomorrow and I said no. I'm just gettin' over it, you know; I'll start likin' him again if we go out, I know it. . . . Yeah, I know he's a jerk, but I still like him.

His girlfriend's so stupid. He cheats on all his girlfriends. He cheated on his last girlfriend with *her.* She should know but she's just blind and stupid. She found out he was kissin' some other girl on prom night and she broke up with him for like, 10 minutes. Then she came crawlin' back. Isn't he a jerk?

*When I was in high school there were a lot of guys who treated the girls terribly—and they kept coming back for more.*

That's me. *(Laughs.)* I can't help it. One night he came to me when I was cryin':

"Why are you crying?"

"You know why I'm crying."

"Well I told you, I'm not gonna break up with her. You can't have me; you can share me."

Can you believe that? What a jerk! But I went back to him.

Sex has a lot to do with it. Most of the girls in my grade have had sex. It's like, if you're datin' a guy you have to, when he's ready. I never have; that's probably why he wouldn't break up with her. He tried to get me to and everything. I'm sure I would have if we were going out. I came pretty close when we were just sneakin' around. I don't think it's right. And I don't wanna get pregnant. No one uses birth control. The guys just don't care about it and the girls can't go on the pill without their parents' permission, and there aren't many parents that'll give it. There aren't any girls that'll even ask. They don't wanna be grounded for the rest of their life.

But most guys are like that. They're not gonna stick around if the girl's not putting out. So I've never been able to keep a relationship for that long. I guess if I want a real relationship I'll just have to do it.

*The high school scene in Delray was a shock for Nelson, 15, who was born and raised in Kansas:*

I have a little brother. In Kansas we lived in a little town. Everything was real cas(ual). Since we moved here, my little brother's changed; he just don't care about nothin'. It's too big for him; there's too much shit happening. People gettin' killed and robbed and whatnot. He just can't deal with it.

We moved here in '87. My dad had to move here for business, but we're going back soon. He really hates it here—he hates the old people. I like the beach, but that's about it. The people are mean. Old ladies freak out 'cause their bill was 50 cents more than they thought it would be. There's a lot of crime. Here we got the black ghetto on Atlantic Avenue. This friend of mine, her husband was driving down Atlantic with his windows rolled up. He stopped at a red light; this black guy comes up and smashes his window with a brick. Then he knocked him out and stole his wallet and his radio.

The middle school I went to last year is right in the middle of it. They got fences and security and everything. It's crazy. People'll cuss you out when you're walkin' out or driving through. There's three crack houses right by the school. There's drug busts every day, shootings, robberies . . . There are no white people outside of the school. It's real strange because it's two minutes away from downtown, the beach, where all the rich people live.

It takes gettin' used to. I was a white kid from Kansas, and then I was in this school in this black neighborhood. Last year they had this thing called Color Day. If you wore a certain color you got beat up. But no one knew what the color was. It was a bunch of Latin guys and big, black guys that made up the color. They'd beat you up. I got lucky; they never touched me when I had the color on. A friend of mine got beat up bad. He was just walkin' down the corridor, and they nailed him in the face and broke his jaw. There were bloodstains on the wall.

*As the interview continued, the thing that struck me about Nelson was his resignation. He didn't gripe about being stuck in Delray—a place he clearly would rather not be—he just made the most of a bad deal. Florida seemed to have numbed him. His only smile came when I asked him about Kansas.*

We're moving back to Kansas in two months. I want to finish growin' up there, graduate from high school. . . . Yeah, it's a lot more relaxed there. You don't have to worry about someone walkin' down the corridor and just smashin' you for no reason. I mean, here you can get beat up by someone you don't even know.

*How else are the people different in Kansas?*

Well, the girls in Kansas are normal girls, you know. Here they're more like hookers, sluts. They act real snobbish and stuff. They look real good; they're all tan and they got good bodies, but they wear so much makeup they look like a . . . makeup kit. Makeup kits with legs.

I think it's, like, one out of every five girls here gets pregnant in high school. It's not surprising—there's a girl in my math class that's always saying, "Hey look!" and pullin' her shirt up. I was at PBCC (Palm Beach Community College) with my dad one night—he works there—and these two drunk girls called to us, and when we looked they pulled their skirts up over their heads and they had nothin' on underneath. That's the way girls are in Florida.

They're so stupid about it too. I mean, nobody ever uses anything. The guys never take any precautions or anything. They get 'em pregnant and they dump 'em. Some girls are startin' to carry condoms around in their purses, but most are like, "Fuck it, I'll just get an abortion."

I don't believe in abortion. It's one thing if a girl gets raped, but if you're doin' it for pleasure, then an abortion's like murder. That's the way my parents feel about it.

*My last interview for the week was with Aretha, 15, a resident of the ghetto mentioned above. I really liked Aretha. She was very calm and direct, and she had a great habit of holding her head at a slight angle and waving her hand slowly from side to side when making a point. I asked her to tell me about her neighborhood and the things that happen there:*

I been livin' there all a my life, so it don't bother me that much anymore, y' get used to it. You just make sure y' house is locked up 'cause they just come in and take everythin' out.

I live right in the middle of Atlantic Avenue—the bad part a town. My parents won't allow me to leave the house at night. They shoot at night and they don't care . . . whoever get hit get hit. You walk outta y' place and BOOM, someone's gettin' shot. You gotta be careful when you walk down the street 'cause they just jump you. Two people have got shot on the side street I live on. It's real scary. It's a dangerous place, I don't like it.

*If I tried to walk Atlantic Avenue from one end to the other, would I make it?*

*(Giggles.)* Don't try it—no, you probably wouldn't make it. If you do, you better bring a *big* gun, or a badge. The cops'll stop any white guy comes into the neighborhood, 'cause they know they're comin' for drugs. Ain't no white people come in the neighborhood 'less they're dealin' or buyin'.

Nah, I don't think there's a real racial problem in Delray Beach; it's the blacks against the blacks and the whites against the whites. The whites live on the beach and we live down here; we're not allowed to go in their area, and they can't come in here. I went to the beach *once,* and I got jumped by four white girls. I was with my mom—she works up there, takin' care of this lady's kids—and I decided to take a walk. My mom says, "OK, just be careful." I was walkin' on the beach, and these four white girls come over, real friendly, like, "Hi, how ya doin'?"

"Fine."

"Well not for long you ain't!"

And then it was *boom, boom,* and that was it. *(Laughs.)* I couldn't do nothin'. I couldn't get no licks in, 'cause they was all bigger than me. That's the last time I've been on the beach.

But man, this neighborhood here's *baaad.* People get shot, robbed, raped—my cousin got raped when she was 13. She's 17 now. She was just goin' to the store—Mama heard her scream—and one a the guys comes in and says, "She got raped!" and we all went out. My cousin didn't even report it to the police. She was like, "They ain't gonna do nothin'." And she's right, 'cause if a black person calls the Delray Beach police, they ain't gonna do nothin'. They gettin' sick and tired a what's happenin' in our neighborhood and they're just lettin' it go. I don't think that's right. They wanna tear the neighborhood down and put up new houses and condominiums and stuff, and I think that's what they should do. My mom doesn't want she should lose the house, but I say, "I'd rather tear down the house than get shot at and raped and all."

Yeah, the police come around, and when they sit there and stay all night everythin's peaceful. But when there's not a cop there you don't never sleep. These guys stay out on the street all night long playin' loud music, fightin' . . . Sometimes when I'm sick—I get sick a lot—my mom goes out and says, "Aretha's sick. Can you keep the music down?" They know me as the quiet girl, and they say, "Oh, that quiet girl, Aretha? Yeah, we can give the quiet girl some quiet." Sometimes I tell my mom to go out and lie and say I'm sick.

There's this one guy, they call him Rock, he's the biggest drug dealer in our neighborhood. He lives just down the street. Everybody works for him—my brother works for him. If he gets mad at his dealers he kills 'em—just like that. Rock likes to take his gun out with him and play with it. He likes to put it in people's faces and slap 'em around. We know that he killed a couple a boys in our neighborhood, but there ain't nobody gonna say nothin', 'cause then he just say, "Yeah, OK, I'll come and get you also." We keep it to ourselves; that's the way it is.

There was one time I was standin' out on the porch when Rock came runnin' by with a gun in his hand. He's chasin' this other guy—I didn't know him. Then I hear a BOOM, and Rock comes runnin' back, throws the gun in his house, and comes sittin' on his porch like nothin' ever happened. I ran in and said, "Mama, Rock just went and shot that boy f' nothin', and she says, "Aretha, you don't say nothin'. If the police ask, you didn't see nothin'." I says, "OK."

*(She pauses for a moment, and I sense she is slightly embarrassed. Embarrassed, I imagine, because she is criticizing her own home. Perhaps she feels that, if there is something wrong with her home, there must be something wrong with her too.)*

The neighborhood wasn't like this until a couple a years ago, when the drugs got real bad. People came into the neighborhood with their drugs and it took the place down. My brother got mixed up in it, and it makes it bad for my family because they come to my house lookin' for my brother and sayin' they gonna shoot up our house because a him. He's dealin' drugs and doin' drugs, and he owes people a lotta money, and that's why they come after him. They tell my mom they better get their money or there ain't gonna be nobody alive in the house in the mornin' when she wakes up. My grandfather says. "Well, I got my gun too, so you best watch out for y'selves."

My brother's 21. We was brought up in the church; we all good people. He just hangs out with the wrong crowd. It's the people you hang around that changes you. We say, "Man, you need help," and he says, "I don't need no help. I got my life under control." My brother's good deep down, but the drugs fucked him up. He'll be real sweet one minute, and then the next he gets all crazy and wants to fight everybody in the house, and his eyes get as red as fire. I'll say, "Man, you high, get away from me," and he'll be like, "I ain't high, I ain't high!" and he'll leave the house and come back later like nothin' ever happened. He's nuts. *(Laughs.)*

I'm tryin' real hard to get outta school. I keep to myself; I don't care about hangin' with the in crowd. I don't wanna get pregnant and drop out of school—there's a lotta that goin' around. Not me. My sister got pregnant at a' early age. She told her boyfriend. She went to his house, and his house was *empty*. He moved completely out.

That's the way it is with black guys—it happens all the time. A white guy, if you go to a white guy and tell 'im you're pregnant, he's gonna stay with you. . . . No, nobody really uses birth control.

*What a strange feeling it was listening to Aretha. We were sitting in the school-yearbook office, with pictures of cheerleaders and flowery poems tacked to the wall, and I thought how bizarre it was that in another hour half the student body would return home to the beach while the other half was dodging bullets—and all of this in a span of less than two miles. In school they all seemed the same.*

*Over the weekend I met the captain of a charter fishing boat and spent a Saturday afternoon enhancing my sunburn while supposedly fishing for kingfish and dolphin. It was so nice to be on a boat that I didn't even flinch each time my line became entangled with those of the other 30 people.*

*I talked to the captain about how things had changed around South Florida in recent years. All the while a pale, scrawny, curly-haired girl named Gilda helped with the bait and the beers and the tangled lines. I assumed she was his daughter, but she wasn't. She was a 16-year-old junior-high dropout who had been helping the captain and his crew for about two years. He said in that time she hadn't said more than a dozen words and that he really didn't know anything about her.*

*I put myself next to her and struck up a conversation about fishing. It wasn't easy. She smiled and said as little as possible—this fish was good to eat, that one was difficult to catch. I became more bold:*

*"By the way, I'm from the principal's office. Why weren't you in school this week?"*

*(Smiles.) I don't think they'd even bother with me. I haven't been in school for a while."*

*"Why not?"*

*"Oh, it's not for me. I'd rather fish."*

*"It's pretty unusual though, don't you think, leaving school so early?"*

*"Well, even when I was there I didn't really do nothin'. So it's better this way. I don't waste anybody's time, and I get to come out here a few times a week."*

*"What do you do on the other days?"*

*"Oh, I make money cleaning and taking care of things for people. Sometimes I sell the fish I catch here to the Haitian ladies that wait on the dock."*

*"What was it you didn't like about school?"*

*"Oh, I just didn't fit in. I don't like doing the things they do—I'm not like them. And I wasn't too good at the work. I failed all my tests. I mean, look at me. I don't care what clothes I'm wearing or about my hair or anything. School was just a waste of time. This is what I like doing."*

*"What about your parents?"*

*"They like the fish I bring home."*

*A moment later the boat was surrounded by dolphin—there must have been a hundred of them—bright yellow and green flashes of light coming to the surface and launching themselves into flight. The boat was in pandemonium.*

*I didn't get the chance to finish my talk with Gilda—I didn't want to pry, anyway. An interesting girl. She seemed just as intelligent as the girls in school, if not more so. She had that quiet self-assurance and aloofness I often found in those whose experience outmeasures their years.*

*At the dock I watched her sell some of her fish to the demented, screaming Haitian women, all of whom seemed willing to kill for the best fish. Gilda surprised me with a story—a legend?—about a captain who had treated one of the Haitian women harshly and who, the story goes, had been placed under a curse. He drowned a short time later.*

*"Do you believe that?" I asked her.*

*"Oh, I don't know. I've seen stranger things."*

*My car was so hot on Monday afternoon that I had to steer all the way to Atlantic High using nothing more than the nail of my pinky. I really don't know how Floridians can bear the heat.*

*I was 10 minutes late for the first interview because a very old woman with blue hair was driving 10 miles an hour in a 40-mile-an-hour zone—a common South Florida occurrence. In the heat of that delay I decided to get more information about Florida's diverse population and it's effect on the state. Burt, a 12-year-old local, summed up the racial situation:*

There's a lot of talk about the racial thing, you know. I'm not prejudiced, but a lot of people are. A lotta people blame the blacks for all the drug problems we got around here, but that's not fair—it's the fuckin' Cubans! They started all that shit. They should just send them home.

*Lena was a very perceptive 15-year-old native of Fort Lauderdale. She said that the massive influx of people was ruining the state, and I asked her to explain why:*

Everyone's pouring into Florida. I feel like we're being invaded. Especially people from Cuba and everything. They're going from one government to another—they're coming into our schools too, and they can't even speak English. It's not only Cubans; there are the Haitians, Jamaicans, Mexicans, PR's. It's tough on the teachers here because they don't know what's going on, and it slows down the whole class. People are just pouring in. They flooded Miami and Fort Lauderdale, and now the smaller places like this are gettin' it.

These people come, there are two choices: They live in poverty like they did in their own country, or they deal drugs. I'm not prejudiced or nothin', but when you see a Cuban driving a sports car, you know how he paid for it. I grew up in Fort Lauderdale, and we didn't have a lot of money. The neighborhood was filled with Cuban drug dealers. It was like *Scarface*. It's changed everything, 'cause drug dealing's become, like, a real job. Everyone's dealin'. Kids were dealin' in my middle school.

Then you have the Americans from New Jersey, New York, Connecticut, Michigan . . . I think they should stay where they are. I mean, it's OK to visit—it's warm and everything—but they come here and stay here. They overcrowd everything.

*(Lena stands and begins to pace, circulating the air with broad gestures. She's worked herself into a frenzy, but she's having fun with it, and she's fun to watch.)*

There isn't much land anymore. There's a building going up on every corner. There's a lot of pollution. Most of these people are old, real old. They come down here to retire, and I guess since they're old they feel they can just mouth off to everybody.

Everybody hates the way the old people drive. They clog up I-95 'cause they drive 35 miles an hour in the fast lane. They slow down *everything.*

A lot of the young people down here feel that the old people should leave, because, like, this is really a young place, with the beach and all the other good stuff. Old people don't belong here.

The college kids are another thing. When I was in Lauderdale that was a problem. They come for Christmas vacation and spring break, and they just destroy the place. They think they own the place. They destroy the hotel rooms, break windows, get into fights. They forget that there's people who live there all year round.

The real bad thing is, all these outsiders have changed the people here. All the drugs coming in, that's changed the people here who wouldn't have nothing to do with drugs if it wasn't brought to 'em like that. But now they're like, "Oh, I guess I'll try this and see what it's like."

Florida hasn't got anything to do with the South anymore. They should just pick it up and move it somewhere else.

*What about th—*

One thing that hasn't changed—sorry for interrupting—is the racial stuff. In South Florida the blacks and the whites pretty much stay with their own people, but the kids mix, in school anyway, and there aren't any problems. I'm not prejudiced, but a lot of people I know are. My dad for instance. He can't stand them. My little sister had a friend down the street that was black—she was about six at the time—and she brought her in to play every now and then. Each time my dad was like, "Why don't you go outside and play?" He tries not to come right out with it, but it's pretty obvious. His whole family's like that. They were all born and raised in Georgia. I've had a lot of black friends that are nice. It's different with the Cubans; I could handle it if they were just coming here on vacation or something, but they're staying and overpowering the place.

I'm not a racist but, I don't know, I could never go out with a black guy. I guess that doesn't sound good. But I like the way the blacks . . . I like their attitude. If they make a friend who's white they try to behave like them and everything. They think a lot about their past. They really get into Martin Luther King. They tell us about it. My black friends sometimes get angry at me and other white kids 'cause we never think about our past. We don't even know about our past. *(Laughs.)* The blacks are really religious too. They go to church and stuff, and they're proud of it. The whites aren't into that—even if they go to church they won't admit it. Like, a popular white kid could never admit that.

*If you wo—*

A lot of the old people here are Jewish. Sorry. They're not . . . nobody likes 'em very much. They're a little worse than the other old people, a little more cranky—and the other ones are *cranky*. In grocery stores—my math teacher's Jewish, and he told us a great joke to play on old Jews in grocery stores. When you're in line, make sure she's not looking, then you put a couple extra items in her basket. You gotta make sure you're ahead of her or else you'll be there for an hour. They go nuts!

Old Jewish ladies on the checkout line at Publix—they got coupons that are like 10 years old. They can't understand it. They watch the cash register. "Forty-nine cents! I'm not gonna pay 49 cents for that! I saw it at Winn Dixie for 48 cents!" Nobody wants to deal with them, 'cause they're never satisfied. In restaurants, they send their food back five times. They talk down to you, and they always blame you for something. They're just plain rude.

*Do you think rudeness is just a part of growing old?*

Well, I think it has to do with losing control. I mean, the young people are making the decisions and the old people are angry 'cause they're losing their power. No, I don't think I'll be like that when I get old. I think I've learned enough from these old people so that I won't be like that. I've already gotten to the point where I just smile and say, "Yes ma'am."

*Our time, one class period, was up. Lena continued to pace, this time begging me to extend the interview so she wouldn't have to go to algebra class. I said that I couldn't. She pleaded. I said no, she was my last interview of the day and I was going home. She made some whining sounds, then mumbled something about algebra having no impact on real life, life outside school. I let her stay on the condition she split her bagged lunch with me, then carry my work things out to the car. I, too, hated algebra.*

*I spoke to several more kids the next day at Atlantic, but their comments were nearly identical to Lena's.*

*My last few days in Delray were spent in auto repair shops—two tires, wheel bearings, new oil pan, and brake pads, all of which, I would find out later, were unnecessary. I left on Mother's Day, May 13, and headed toward Jacksonville, the first stop on the Florida–Massachusetts leg of my journey.*

*As I started out I was again thinking about the lack of regional differences in the towns I had visited. How nice it would be to find a place with its own special identity; a place where the buildings and the landscape and the people and the things the people did and ate and drank were the inextricable ingredients of a unique atmosphere. That's what I hoped to find. Was there any such place? Were there any kids who still reflected their town and their history and their parents and not McDonald's and Nintendo and MTV?*

# 6

# Charleston, South Carolina

*It was actually a nice feeling to be back on I-95 after two weeks of relative stability. I felt almost at home that first night at the Motel 6 in Jacksonville. I transcribed some interviews, ate some beer-battered shrimp, monitored CNN, slept, eggs Benedict at Denny's, coffee to go.*

*Passing through Georgia the next morning I amused myself with the local radio. Bible Belt radio is at once irritating and entertaining—24-hour-a-day religious programming. I set my radio to "scan," giving me five seconds on each channel. There was no music: "But with the glory of God we will overcome! We will overcome! And we will". . . . "And Jesus knew he had been deceived, but he opened his arms and welcomed his enemies" . . . "For we are all sinners! And we will all burn in hell if" . . . "And at Emmaus Jesus showed himself again and shared this frugal meal. . . ."*

*I drove through to Charleston, where a friend's friend had promised to introduce me to some parents. Charlestonians actually let you into traffic—they even smile when they're doing it. I responded by smiling back and looking around for other drivers to let in myself. It put me in such a good mood that I splurged on a Best Western in the middle of town. Fifty bucks or so with the five-dollar business discount I received when I flashed someone else's business card. This was a big step from Super 8's and Motel 6's, which can still be gotten for 20 bucks. I felt I was going places.*

*The old part of Charleston, including the harbor, is one of the prettiest places in America. The three-story colonial houses with multi-level roofs and cone-hatted towers, the city buildings with their imposing columns, the narrow, winding cobblestone streets in the commercial area, and the juxtaposition of this old American architecture, which I always associate with New England, and the swaying palm trees that line the streets give Old Charleston the timeless, dreamy quality of a fairy tale.*

*As I was walking down to the harbor, an old man—he must have been 70—came bicycling in my direction at a good clip. Ten yards before me he suddenly veered off, spread-eagled his legs, and glided through a deep puddle, a wide smile on his face. This is the image that still comes to mind when I think of Charleston. It's a place where kids are not only free to be kids, but free to remain that way for the rest of their lives.*

*I arrived in Charleston eight months after the devastation of Hurricane Hugo, and though business was back to normal, a great deal of damage and debris had yet to be swept away. I walked on Folly Beach and saw chairs, tables, and a variety of garage-sale effects in piles every 50 yards. Piers and lifeguard stands remained stacks of defeated lumber, marking the spots where new ones would be erected.*

*Eight months after its arrival, Hugo was still the talk of the town. The souvenir shops had been transformed into Hugo shrines. There were Hugo postcards, Hugo posters, Hugo bed linens, Hugo coffee mugs, Hugo flatware, and, my favorite, Hugo cufflinks, a pair of which I recently wore to a friend's wedding.*

*I talked to 10 kids in Charleston. All of their parents worked in the same office in jobs ranging from secretary to boss. Tracy, a toothy little nine-year-old, recalled the worst of Hugo:*

I was in the house when Hugo hit. The worst part was before it. We were boarding up the house and everything, and I was like, "Wow, I'm gonna die!" When it came, we were in the den, and the window broke—man, that was scary. My dad put plastic over the other windows. It sounded like a big ol' train comin' through. Things were flyin' all over the place. I only looked out once at the beginning, before we covered the windows, and the trees were all going the wrong way, garbage was flyin' around. . . .

We went out when we were in the middle, the eye, just for a minute. It was all calm, real weird, real creepy. Two girls in my class got their houses wrecked.

Something good came out of it though. My dad works in construction some of the time, and he got a lot of money from Hugo. He's, like, fixin' to retire.

*I went to see Cathy, 10, at her house on James Island. Most of the drive from the Best Western was on a single road with beautiful, arching live oaks on either side that left just enough space overhead for the sun to come through.*

*Cathy was another professional kid; her mother was a psychology teacher, her father an English teacher. Cathy, her house, and her family were everything great about the South. When I walked in, her mother offered me a mint julep. Cathy and I went out to the back porch for the interview—it was the kind of hot southern back porch that makes you want to grab a towel and swab the back of your neck—and after forcing the dogs into the yard, she took her place in the hammock with an iced tea.*

*Cathy had a captivating accent that turned "homeroom" into "huhmroom," "hers" into "huhs," and "Charleston" into "Chahlstun."*

My homeroom teacher's a social-studies teacher and he's always right. He came in a few days before Hugo and he said this hurricane was gonna hit us. He went to the weather people, and he came back and showed us how to take care of ourselves with a first-aid kit and how to do supplies and stuff, and it really helped—'cause we had to get out of here in a hurry. We got out of school on Wednesday, and they canceled school for the rest of the week, 'cause everybody had to get out of Charleston. My Mom and my sister and me left Wednesday afternoon. My dad was supposed to meet us on Thursday; he had to stay by himself and take care of our seven dogs and board up all the windows, secure the whole house. We were gonna stay too, but we watched the news Wednesday night, and they just said, "Get out!" I didn't hardly have nothin': a nightgown, a toothbrush . . . We went to Columbia. My dad called us there and said that he got caught up in traffic and that he only made it to Saint Matthews, which is like two hours away from Columbia—but he was only saying that, 'cause he didn't want to make my mom nervous; he was calling from our house; he was never gonna leave. He wanted to watch over the house. He stayed in the long closet in their bedroom. He had an air mattress and a sleeping bag, television, telephone, cat, and he had all the dogs secured in the garage. We didn't find any of this out until the morning, because he was afraid my mother would be worried. He explained that even if a tree crushed the house he would've been all right, because he was lying on his back in the closet—no tree could have smashed all the way through the house.

After the storm he went outside. The first thing he saw was that the big tree from the front yard was halfway into my sister's room—I'm lucky 'cause my room is right next to hers—just about everything in her room was ruined. There was another tree that crushed the garage and a lot of broken windows and stuff. It was paid by insurance.

The whole neighborhood was just completely destroyed. The people across the street had a freezer full of frozen chickens, and they had to cook for everybody 'cause there was no utilities for like a week.

There was a house on Folly Beach that got destroyed, and when they started clearing the rubble away they found a porpoise—in the house! They took a door and they strapped the porpoise onto it and set it off to sea.

*(Cathy goes into the kitchen and brings back two fresh iced teas. She insists I take the hammock for the remainder of the interview. I have a hammock, half a mint julep, an iced tea, and a bowl of homemade oatmeal raisin cookies. I have never been so comfortable.)*

We came back about two weeks later—Dad said there were trees zigzagging across the roads, so we waited until they were clear—and the place was still a mess! There were trees all over the place, lines were down, there was no electricity, no nothing. I have this friend, Betty, down the street who stayed through the storm, and I went to see her as soon as I got back. There were three big trees right on top of her house. I was so scared—she had scars all over her legs from where she tripped over some wires and stuff, and they had to move because their house was all rubble.

There was no telephones, TV, electricity for three weeks. It was terrible. I have a friend who lives in the country on a dirt road; she didn't get her lights back for three months! There was a house the next road over and it was just split right in half by a tree.

There was a lot of looting in the stores and stuff, so we had a curfew—all of Charleston—where we couldn't go out or drive around past eight or something.

*What did you do? No lights, power, no school . . .*

We helped around the neighborhood—that's what everybody did. It was really kinda fun. We picked up branches, we fixed up our yard, we helped people move things around—those people who were leaving—we helped them pack up. At night we read books with candles. We did a lot of scavenger hunting. When we got our phones back on, there must have been a hundred phone calls. There's a boy I know who lives in Folly Beach, and he was in the newspapers because he gathered so much stuff from the beach: wash machines, sewing machines, china, beds, all kinds of things.

This porch is new. We were thinking, "If there's gonna be bulldozers all around, why don't we get a new porch?"

For five months all anyone ever talked about was Hugo. Hugo this, Hugo that. It's still like that a little. I'll ask a friend if she still has her red purse and she'll say, "No, I lost it during Hugo."

*Hugo must have changed a lot of people—it makes you think that anything can happen.*

It changed everybody. All of a sudden, if there was a tornado warning the whole city would clear out; if it started raining hard everyone would think the floods were gonna carry us away. The whole thing was really strange; God took a quiet, peaceful place like Charleston and just picked it up and shattered it all over the place.

*For Cathy's sister, Kim, five at the time of Hugo, the storm was more of a personal inconvenience:*

No, I didn't like Hugo. I had to move into my sister's room 'cause everything in mine got smashed. We hated sharing the same room—we fighted all day long.

*She thought Hugo a normal thing. Like most healthy five-year-olds, Kim spent a good bit of time in her own world, where hurricanes are never a threat. On my way out she suddenly appeared in a neon blue leotard with frilly things on the neck and wrists and demanded I stay until she sang and danced two numbers from her upcoming grammar-school theatrical debut.*

*I stopped on my way home in a sports bar/restaurant for dinner, looking forward to sitting down to a cold beer and some fish while watching the Boston Bruins playoff game I had been excited about all day. Immediately I fell in with the bartender and the other guys at the bar, who took me right into their conversation. When game time came I reminded them of the event and the channel. They stared at me, then laughed. "This is South Carolina. What the hell do we care about ice hockey?" Nice people. But no sense of priorities.*

*I met Gwen, 10, the next day. She was a bundle of kinetic energy. In the small room where we talked, she managed to jump, run, hang and vault:*

Sundays are big days around here. We go to church a lot—AME, African Methodist Church, African Methodist Episcopal Church. Now the thing is, see, every time I go there and there's a sermon—I don't even know what he's talkin' about! And you have to sit there, and it seems like it's a few hours before it's through.

*(She raises her arms and screams/groans, as if in urgent need of help.)* That's what it's like. I don't understand a word of it!

There's one preacher I like; you can understand him. He tells funny stories. He doesn't do all that wild stuff, jumpin' around, like my regular preacher does.

*It gets pretty hot in those churches, doesn't it?*

*Maaaan,* you shoulda seen it yesterday. I was an usher—it was hot! I was just sittin' there, sneaking candy outta my purse, and my shirt was stuck to me, I was sweatin'—and the preacher!, he was like *(flails her arms), "Aaahhhhh! Oooooooo! Yeeeaaahhh!"* Man, sweat was just *pourin'* offa him. I don't listen to him, but he's fun to watch. He was talkin' about love and fear: "If God's love abides in you, you shouldn't have any fear . . ." I've been in a couple a mixed churches, black and white, and they're the most fun churches. It's not as serious. They don't have to sit there all the time. They've got, like, separate buildings where the kids go. They spend most the time seein' movies and eatin' popcorn.

When we're not in church we're at Sunday school. That's not so bad when you're smart like me; I know just how to make it look like I'm payin' attention. I sneak a lotta candy.

Every Sunday we have a big dinner at my grandmother's, the whole family. Last night we had turkey wings, apple pie, macaroni-and-cheese; she had beef with gravy, she had potatoes, she had cake— she *knows* how to buy food and she *knows* how to cook it.

*Last night I had grits for the first time in my life. It tastes like something you should be using to repair the hurricane damage—and down here you eat it every day—it comes with whatever you order in restaurants. Why?*

*(Laughs.) Maaaan,* you can tell you're not from South Carolina. It tastes *good.* Everyone loves grits. When you go out to eat you get grits on your plate, instead a like, rice or somethin'. I love grits. I hate sausage—you probably love it.

*What's the story with the iced tea; there are two different kinds . . .*

That's sweetened or unsweetened. You gotta tell 'em which kind you want. Man, you can tell you don't come from South Carolina.

*Her brother Derick, 16, was more serious:*

Yeah, Charleston's a real friendly place, and it's changed a lot from the way it was in the '60s. I've never had any problem, but there *is* racism in our school. We protested on Martin Luther King's birthday because we had to go to school—we don't usually have to—on account of Hugo. Hurricane Hugo. Everybody was all upset about that, but we came because we missed so much school after Hugo hit. Then a couple a months later here comes George Washington's birthday or someone like that, and we didn't have to come to school. So we were like, "What's goin' on here?" and we got together and had an assembly in the school hall. All the black people in the school wore black clothes to show our protesting.

There's a lot of blacks and whites that hang together in school—things are usually pretty cool—it's just once in a while something like that happens.

*Back on James Island I talked to Candy, a ponytailed 12-year-old, in the sunny, New Kids on the Block-filled room she shared with her younger sister. It was a fairy-tale room with giant stuffed animals and flouncy lace curtains that blew into the room with the breeze:*

I don't mind sleeping with my little sister; it's kinda fun. We got our own rooms when my brother moved out, but we got lonely so we moved back in. He came back anyway. My sister and me are gonna live together when we get older. Not in the same room, the same place.

We both like the same things. We hate scary movies, the bloody ones. We *love* Freddy Krueger—you know, *Nightmare on Elm Street*. I've seen part 1, part 2, part 3, part 4, and I gotta see part 5.

*But those are scary movies.*

Yeah but, it's not scary once you see it over and over and over again. I've memorized all the parts; I know exactly what's gonna happen so it doesn't scare me. But the first time you see it, that gets you. I've seen part 2 about a thousand times. My favorite part is where that girl turned into a roach—at the very beginning she had a sandwich, and Freddy Krueger knew that she hated roaches, so he put one in her sandwich and she screamed, and at the end she turned into a roach.

I love Freddy. I seen 'im in real life—not in real life but in TV—without Freddy's mask on. He doesn't look scary or nothin'. But he's not cute. *(Laughs.)*

The other ones scare me. There's this other movie that was sometimes scary, sometimes funny. There was this lady dancing, and her bones—her head fell off and she was holdin' it . . . and we saw this other movie about this real bad teacher, and one night they did this devil spell on 'im and so they pulled this old person's hand out of the grave—out of the mix—and that made his head fall off; and he was walkin' around with it and they were gettin' 'im, and holdin' on to 'im . . . that one was real scary, I didn't like it. Sometimes you can tell that it's fake, and then it's OK, but the real ones, the ones that are like, *real,* I don't like them.

*Are there any things that scare you in real life?*

Sometimes I get scared when I'm home all alone and I think some guy's tryin' to get in—I saw a ghost in here once! It was a woman and she was floatin' on the ceiling—it was 6:30 and I was eatin' my cereal and she came floatin' on the ceiling on top a me, watchin' me eat, and I screamed and took my bowl a cereal and knocked on my mom and dad's door and ate in with them. My mom saw the lamp shake; she said so. I saw it with my own eyes.

*Have there been any other extraterrestrial sightings in the house?*

Well, if I have to tell you, there was this man who blew off his head in the utility room. It was before we moved here; the neighbors told us about it. This guy had so much stress, one day he took his kids to school, and he had too much stress on 'im, so he went to the utility room and blew off his head. His wife came back and saw him bleedin' to death and she stuck her fist down his throat to stop him from bleedin' and he died.

And there was a woman that died in my mom's room before we moved in—I think it was her that I saw floatin' on the ceiling. Sometimes my sister gets bad nightmares, and that's why we keep these Bibles under our pillows. *(On both beds, under both pillows, are Gideon Bibles. She shows me hers, then tucks it back in. She places her pillow on the Bible, her head on the pillow.)* We like to have them there if we watch scary movies or somethin'; people say that really helps. You're supposed to sleep with your head on the Bible so God will protect you from bad dreams.

*Nat, nine, was upset because his father had yelled at him for dragging his muddy feet through the white kitchen floor. He looked up at me with glazed "I didn't mean to do it" eyes:*

I know it was my fault. Sometimes you don't think about those things. Sometimes I get into trouble at school. Some paper towels stopped up the sink in the boys' room, and the water came out on the floor . . . I did it . . . I guess it was pretty stupid. I had to go to the principal's office.

*How do you think your parents really feel about you?*

I know they like me. I know when I get into trouble and they yell at me they don't really mean it, not for long anyway. But they got real mad about the toilet thing.

I gotta clean up my room now. 'Cause every time my parents are mad at me, I clean up my room and it makes them happy again.

*I left Charleston after four days. Charleston had everything I had hoped to find in the South—just the kind of place I envisioned in Florida—and my euphoric four days washed away the sour memories of Missouri and Alabama.*

*I was surprised to find that despite television and satellites there really are some regions of the United States that have their own special identity for all the right reasons. I was also surprised to find that some kids in some places think the same things I did 16 years ago. Sixteen years ago, in the second grade, I spent an hour crying in Douglas Chandler's office after stopping up the sink in the boys' room and flooding the floor.*

# 7

# Hightstown, New Jersey

*I spent a night with relatives in Charlotte, then drove through to my hometown of East Brunswick, New Jersey, arriving on May 20. This marked the beginning of a month spent on couches in friends' apartments throughout the Northeast. Fortunately for me, many of my old friends still lived alone, and I used their kitchens and warmed their telephones without the hesitation I would have felt in the presence of a roommate or spouse. Freeloading is always permitted under such conditions.*

*Many of these friends were women—high-school girls the last time I had seen them. A word about women in their 20s who live alone: Ninety-five percent of them own cats, most of these yet to be declawed. I suppose cats help ward off loneliness, but I learned to my surprise that these animals provide a measure of protection as well. These are vicious, carnivorous beasts capable of great destruction. From New Jersey to Boston they pounced on me at obscene hours of the morning, as if to express their displeasure with my presence. We wrestled and clawed.*

*At any rate, it proved interesting to visit childhood friends while writing a book about children. I saw how much we all had changed; how our environment and the trends of our time had influenced us. All through my youth I was slightly bitter about living where we did. East Brunswick is a generic suburb, peopled with New York City commuters, where nothing ever happens. I was bitter that I didn't live in a more exciting place where I could have seen and experienced more. Like the girl in Houston, Minnesota, I yearned for something more.*

*I spent five years at the Peddie School in Hightstown, New Jersey. We were all prototypical professional kids there. We felt omniscient despite our youth and inexperience, and quite confident we would conquer the world. The school preached the standard American prep-school philosophy: SAT scores, college interviews, extracurricular activities and sports for the sake of college transcripts, college, entry-level position, wife, promotion, money . . . there was a stress factor in that, especially for those like me who didn't find the philosophy attractive. There was also a lot of partying.*

*My friends told me that Peddie had eliminated partying by instituting a one-strike-you're-out rule with regard to drugs and alcohol. I couldn't imagine it. I went there and talked to some of the eighth graders, all of them 14, the youngest kids in the school. Having little free time, they brought sandwiches with them and met me during their lunch periods.*

*The place looked the same: a sea of blue-and-white striped Oxford-cloth shirts, penny loafers, side parts, L. L. Bean book bags. I sat and talked to the kids in the very same algebra classroom where, years before, I had suffered beyond measure.*

*Mitch had bologna and cheese on Wonder bread with mustard. Despite his heartiness, he managed to swallow only a portion of his sandwich; the rest either clung to his braces or flew in my direction. Mitch was very short and very loud:*

*Some years ago I was an eighth grader in this place. Everybody looked at us as being babies.*

Especially for me. I'm five feet tall, exactly. I don't really mind being short. I'd like to be tall—I hope I do grow—but being short's OK too. I just laugh at the short jokes; they don't bother me.

But I took care of the eighth-grade-baby thing because I have the biggest mouth. I mean, by myself I could probably outscream this entire school. A lot of kids hate my guts here 'cause I scream at them when they pick on me. One time some sophomores threw me into a garbage can and put the lid on so I couldn't get out. I started screaming, and eventually the janitor heard me. I don't remember what I did exactly; it could have been anything. I don't know why, but I always end up mouthing off to the big kids and then they take care of me. I once got in a fight with this real big kid—he's on the football team and everything—he's really, really fat. I sat down and he pushed me, to take my seat, and I said, "Get out of my seat," and he said, "Make me," and I said, "I can't unless you go on a diet, you fat tub of lard." He picked me up and he *threw* me against a brick wall.

By being a loudmouth you can back yourself into a corner, but you can also keep people away from you—those people you don't want getting too close. There's a kid in the eighth grade that gets picked on a lot, and he just whines when they do, so they pick on him more. Me, I'll start screaming and scratching—I fight back. Yesterday on center campus we were playing this game, and one of the seniors kept knocking me in the mouth, and my braces were cutting into my lips. I got fed up, so I just hit him back, and he stopped messing with me. People don't expect you to fight back, especially when you're short and skinny.

People pick on me for so many different reasons; they pick on me just because I'm so short—so many times I've been called a "short shit." They think that's really funny. I just say, "Well I may be short but you're ugly, and I can always grow." Then they turn around and deck me.

There was a freshman last week at soccer practice who started with the "short shit" thing. I said, "Go to hell, you stupid asshole." After practice I walked up to the student center, and when I turned the corner he just nailed me. *(Mitch pounds the side of his fist against the table to demonstrate the severity of his beating. In doing so, he splashes a puddle of Gulden's mustard on me and my tape recorder.)*

Because of my mouth I have a lot of seniors on my side—I'm the only eighth grader they know. They had this thing where the eighth graders were supposed to go to the chapel and try to sing the school song louder than the seniors. I was the only one that showed up. And I almost beat them. Everyone else chickened out. They carried me back to the student center on their arms, and for the next week I had all senior privileges; I got to sit in the senior lounge, senior lunch line . . . So because of my mouth the seniors respect me—the whole thing has a lot to do with having some balls. I take a licking and keep on ticking.

I'm the only person who doesn't mind taking speech and drama classes. The only time I get embarrassed is in restaurants, when my dad tries to pick up waitresses for me. But that's it.

. . . Yeah, I guess I am an A-type person. I'm gonna be a sports agent; I'll try to negotiate big contracts for athletes. It's a good way to use my big mouth. There's big money involved, and it won't be hard for me to get into it. When I want something I go and get it—I don't usually fail. That's why I'm gonna be a success. I *know* I'm gonna be successful after college, because that's what I want, that's why I'm in this school. You've gotta be prepared—that's what separates you from the others when it comes to getting out in the real world.

*I got a chill during that last paragraph. I had a great urge to demand that he chase girls or stop up the school toilet—anything! Fourteen-year-old kids concerned with balancing checkbooks make me nervous.*

*Next was Bob, an American patriot who used more clichés than all my other interviewees combined. He had roast beef with lettuce and tomato and ketchup on whole wheat, which he ate slowly and with great precision. He only took a bite when I was talking, and didn't speak until he had swallowed:*

I think discipline is a real important thing to have—that's why I like going to private school instead of public school. They leave you to make a lot of decisions for yourself, and that builds up discipline. You need discipline. I mean, it's a dog-eat-dog world out there.

I'm looking forward to a career in the military. My dad was a marine. My grandmother was one of the first WAVES. She flew Hellcats to the flattops in the Pacific, to deliver them. I had three uncles killed in World War II: one in the Battle of Britain, one on Iwo Jima, and one in the Battle of the Bulge. I had two relatives that died fighting in the Spanish-American war. My father was real close to being a lifer, so you can see that the military is real important to us.

*How would you feel about going into combat?*

That wouldn't bother me. I read a lot about it. You get in there and you do what you have to do. It's just a shame that the whole country doesn't feel that way anymore. During the Second World War everybody was pitching in; during Vietnam the soldiers were coming home after fighting for their country and people were calling them baby killers. I'm not a dove or a hawk—I just think that when the country, the government makes a decision, you have to stand by it. . . . Yes, of course I'd have gone to Vietnam. I have no problem with dying for my country.

*What do you think of the people who dodged the draft?*

Well, that's just cowardice. You've got to do your duty. There's just no excuse for going to Canada or something. I like the Israelis; I think they handle things the right way. They're protecting their native ground. They've been through a holocaust; the Palestinians are trying to take away their land . . . they do what it takes. If it takes putting a satchel charge on your back and running into a hotel, then that's what it takes. That's the way it should be. The whole nine yards.

I mean, of course you try talking first, but you've got to be ready to shoot. You get much further with a kind word and a gun than you do with just a gun.

*War has changed over the years. It's not glorious like it used to be. The whole thing about coming home a hero—do you think there's anything romantic about it anymore?*

Values have deteriorated; the laws of war don't count anymore. They shoot at anybody . . . chemical weapons. . . . No, it's not as romantic as it used to be . . . like the Flying Leathernecks.

*Do you think our country is still as powerful as it was?*

No. I think America has gone soft. The average American is overweight; the average kid watches too much TV; drugs . . . people are rich and fat and they have no morals; nothing counts except for the almighty dollar. There are still some good eggs but . . . I'm darned if I know what to do about it. I guess a war or a depression are the only things that could wake us up. Like World War II. That was a war. They were threatening our country. If we didn't fight like hell my mother would be opening her door and it would have been like, "Hello, fraulein." That's why it was such a great war to fight in: It was desperate, a war to the finish. There was honor there on all sides. When it comes down to it, it's just killing, but it's very, very nice killing.

*Frankie, the strong, silent type. Ham and swiss, mustard and mayonnaise, kaiser roll:*

My grandparents on both sides come from Italy. My dad's real Italian. He wears a lot of gold, wears a lot of those Cavaricci pants. We have big dinners with the whole family: homemade pizza, lasagna, big bowls of spaghetti—real Italian stuff.

I like being Italian—all Italians do—it's good to be proud of your nationality, or your roots or whatever. There's a lot of people missing that whole part of life.

I kinda like the Mafia. It's kinda exciting, all Italians and everything, the code of silence. I like the way the Italian people stick together, they take care of their own. I'm sure my father would side with Fama just 'cause he's Italian.

That whole case with Yusuf Hawkins bothers me—I come from a real Italian family. The blacks just march through Bensonhurst, they make Bensonhurst out to be like, a crazy place with a lot of crime, they make all Italians out as criminals. I know the kid got jumped and everything, and the guys who did it should be punished, but not every single Italian should be punished, and that's what happens when all the black people march through Bensonhurst. People get jumped all the time, in every neighborhood. I hate it when people go after Italians.

I guess that's just the way it is. People love to pick on other people. Just after Yusuf Hawkins came the Koreans, that lady getting beat up just because she owned a grocery store in the black area. In a way it would almost be better if every group kept to themselves, if they all stayed in the neighborhood.

That's the way I want to live. I want to have my own family, and the rest of my family around me. That's the way Italians are. That's what would make me happy: a good job, a family at home in a nice house. . .

*I can't help but compare these kids with myself and my old friends from the Peddie School. They are not at all as we were. The difference is one of direction. Mitch, Bob, and Frankie share a narrow, constricted vision of their futures, not open to interpretation. They accept their vision and direct their lives toward its realization. Mitch will be a sports agent; Bob will go military; Frankie will live the quiet life. Kids today are simply focused and directed in their images of what the future holds for them.*

*As I said above, my Peddie friends and I were confident we'd conquer the world, but few of us knew exactly how we'd go about doing it, and many of us are still wondering. We recoiled from the pressure of SAT's and college placement. Our visions were more obscure; we dreamed not of marriage or precedent-setting business maneuvers, but of high romance and Glad bags stuffed with cash.*

*Perhaps Mitch, Bob, Frankie, and all the other visionaries I met are the newest link in a logical progression: the lost generation, the me generation, and now the professional generation.*

# 8

# Bristol, Connecticut

*Bristol, Connecticut, is the perfect place to spend the Memorial Day weekend. A pleasant combination of small houses, big houses; old families, new families; lower-middle class and upper-middle class with a sprinkling of the rich and good ol' boys makes Bristol a remarkably self-contained middle-of-the-road northeastern town. It seems the entire population works in some aspect of construction. I met people who cleared brush and provided lumber, people who designed and built houses, and people who sold them. I felled a tree with a chainsaw during my stay. Another first.*

*Family names go back a long way in Bristol—some as far back as the founding of the town. As they say, "Everyone knows the town like the back of his hand." Perhaps this is why the town lacks accurate street signs—or any street signs, for that matter. For example, there's a five-way intersection near the hospital where, as far as I can tell, three streets have the right of way. In lieu of street signs and traffic lights, drivers use hand signals, or often just a smile or a lift of the chin. The latter two methods take practice.*

*An old friend of mine, Cliff, had recently moved to Bristol after marrying into a very robust, Italian house-building family to whom barbecuing was not merely a Sunday activity but a way of life. The holiday weekend was spent gorging on barbecued chicken, ribs, Italian sausages, and desserts beyond description.*

*During one of these barbecues I talked to some of the kids. They were full of life—as spicy and gratifying as the food. My favorite was Paul, a six-year-old, who I'm sure will one day be a great writer of fiction. A notorious teller of tales, Paul is already a gifted improviser. Unfortunately, his stories never lasted more than 30 seconds. Our interview was interrupted after just a few minutes when a garden snake slithered onto the back porch. All the kids went bananas, and it was some time before the interview could be resumed, and then only briefly:*

I've seen bigger snakes than that. I've seen snakes that were bigger than I was, and they were made all of gunk. I've seen cobras before that were so big they could kill elephants.

*I slew a snake a few weeks ago and it was as big as your house. It was a boa constrictor and it was made of gunk. I wrestled it for about six hours until I finally killed it.*

*(An impressed silence.)* Connecticut is full of dinosaurs. I've seen a few. I didn't fight any because if you leave them alone they won't bother you. One of them bothered me once though, and so I rubbed his belly and he fell asleep. That's a trick I know.

*The interview went on like that for a while. When I left a short time later I saw Paul talking to some neighborhood kids on the street. They were gathered around him in a semicircle, and he was telling them my lie about the boa constrictor I battled to the death. The kids were spellbound. One of them asked, "Was it poisonous?" to which Paul, without missing a beat, replied, "I know it was poisonous, because I saw it get bit by a poisonous grasshopper. Once that happens one drop of poison from the snake can kill 50 men." I remember thinking, "This kid is gonna go places."*

*Through Cliff's wife I met a teacher at one of Bristol's Catholic schools, St. Joseph's, and she arranged for me to interview those kids whose parents returned the necessary release form. I was amazed at the response: About 80 percent of the forms were returned. Over three days I interviewed more than 60 kids, all of them clad in uniform green. I never experienced such a diversity of subject and opinion. In this school, drugs were not spoken of, sex was still* Playboy, *and gangs hung out in tree houses, so we talked about other things.*

*Wilona, 13, was addicted to Blistex. She couldn't last five minutes before reaching for the tube and covering the lower third of her face with the lip balm. Between applications she talked about her future:*

I'm gonna marry someone rich and stay home all day. Shopping all the time, soap operas, country club—luxury—that's what I want. I want to spend half my time at the club and the other half at home.

I'd wake up just before my husband went to work. . . . No, the maid would make him breakfast—I don't know how to cook—don't want to learn. I'd just wake up to say good-bye to him. Around two the soaps start: "Guiding Light," "As the World Turns"—those are the ones I'd *have* to watch. Then I'd go off to the country club and do the country-club things—golf, tennis, cards, drinks—then I'd go back home and go out to dinner with my husband.

I know there are lots of people who think that's terrible, to marry someone to live like that. Women's lib ladies would be like, "Oh, women don't do that anymore. We have careers, blah, blah, blah." I think they've gone too far. I think it's terrible that these women drop their kids off at the day-care center every day and pick them up 10 hours later. I think that a woman's place is in the home, raising the children.

The whole country-club thing is in my family. I guess it's pretty popular in Connecticut, especially in the real rich places like Bridgeport. My dad spends more time at the country club than he does at home. He does a lot of business there too. It's a pretty yuppie place.

My dad's even got a girlfriend—my parents are divorced—that

works at the club. She's a waitress there. I don't like her a bit. She's got an attitude problem. I know she's just using my dad for his money. That's how the whole relationship started: She was in financial problems and he helped her out. I think he helps her out with her house that she has—we go to stay at her house on the weekends sometimes. They want to spend time together away from the club, because, you know, she's a waitress there.

The money thing is also in the family. We like to shop and go out to eat and have nice things. I don't have an allowance or anything. When I need some money, I ask my dad, and he usually just gives it to me. I don't see him that often. I asked him if I could have a credit card when I turned 16, but he said no. Probably better that way; I'd have max'ed it out on the first day.

*How are you going to find a rich man to marry?*

I'll go to college for a while.

*When you find him, and you get that gold card, what are some things you'd like to come into possession of?*

Well, a cherry red convertible; white house with black shutters and a big garden, 'cause I like working in gardens; maid; butler; a nice little boat in Essex; and a lot of clothes and shoes.

*Veronica, 10, was made of more humble stuff. She reminded me of Hardy's Tess, an innocent milkmaid. I imagined her putting in long hours at the skimmer and saying her prayers before bed:*

My family's Polish. My mom and dad grew up in Warsaw. They have real thick Polish accents when they speak English. My mom will get upset about something and say, "Hey! Give me the break!" instead of "Give me *a* break."

I go to a Polish school on Saturday. They teach us all this stuff about Poland, and we practice our reading and writing. All of us could speak Polish before we went to the school. I still say my prayers in Polish, because I was saying them back when Polish was the only language I spoke. Hail Mary's are much easier to do in Polish than they are in English.

I've been to Poland four times. The food's really terrible. It's hard over there. The stores don't have anything, and the prices are so high. You have to wait in line for hours to get bread.

The people are nice. It's strange at first, though, because they're wearing these terrible clothes, and they look like bums, some of them. They smell a little too, because they don't take as many showers as we do. They're greedy too, because of waiting on line and the government and everything. My parents say it's much better now than it was when they were young. Kinda hard to believe.

My dad's family is real poor. It's disgusting where they live. There's flies all over the place. The whole house smells like pigs. That's what they do, they raise pigs, and they have horses because they don't have cars. And you know what happens when you have a lot of horses around. *(Veronica unties her long, long brown hair, and it falls around her, engulfing the table.)*

It's weird, talking to my cousins that I have in Warsaw. I help them feed the pigs or whatever, and my cousin—she's almost the same age I am—she talks to me about her dolls, her school work, and how she's gonna help with the farm. It's completely different from over here. My friends here talk about their clothes and their shoes—all the things they have—and my Polish friends talk about their work, because they don't have really anything. My mom got a watch—just a normal watch—for my cousin the last time we went over there, and she went to school like, "Wow, look at this! My American aunt bought me this American watch!" All the kids gathered around her; she was so proud of it. They all think America's the greatest place in the world because everybody has all these great things. Wherever I went there were lots of kids that wanted to hang around with me.

*How do you think your friends over here would handle it if they were suddenly moved into your cousins' school in Poland?*

*(Laughs.)* They couldn't handle it. My friends—they can't even *think* about leaving their house without half a can of hairspray on their heads. I guess American kids are really spoiled. They don't know much about other places, how people live in different coun-

tries. They don't know how good they have it. I was the only one in geography class who knew where Poland was on the map. I guess American kids are really . . . what's the word . . . yeah, ignorant.

So it's good for my family here. My dad's the boss in a factory in New Britain, where the Polish people are, and we have a nice house and everything. We couldn't have that in Poland. They talk sometimes about moving back to Poland—'cause that's their home—but, like, then it would be all pigs and horses. It would be hard to give up all the luxury we have.

*In the middle was Miles, 13:*

The homeless people bother me. They just stay out on the streets; it's like they don't even try to get off. I think they should get a haircut, go down to McDonald's, get a part-time job, and get some money for themselves. Do their own thing.

I feel sorry for them and everything—they might be out on the street because they couldn't pay hospital bills or they lost their job—but I think they gotta *do something* to try and recover. I can't, like, respect people that don't try to get out of their problems.

*To add to the diversity there was Rupert, 12, the most frightening kid I interviewed on my trip—an extremely troubled boy. He was quiet at first, then almost frenetic. All the while he had a mischievous twinkle in his eyes—ice-blue eyes set deep in their sockets:*

I do a lot of dumb things. Sometimes I do them on purpose, for fun, and sometimes they happen by accident. The other day me and my friend were fishing, and when we were on our way back home we passed the big drainpipe—you know, the sewer thing—and we went into it to see what was there. It was kinda like a challenge to each other. It went a long way. We couldn't see anything until we got to the gutters, but we could feel all kinds of spider webs and stuff. We had to crawl some of the way, and when we got out the bottoms of my pants were all wet. I told my mom I fell down when we were fishing. Then the next day I got this real ugly rash all over my knees and I had to go to the doctor. So I guess that was a pretty stupid thing to do.

I get grounded a lot; I get into a lot of trouble. But it's kinda fun. Just a few weeks ago I got grounded for messing with my little brother. He was bothering me and he wouldn't quit, and we were in the kitchen, so I just put my hand around this big knife and looked at him like Freddy Krueger, and he flipped out and went crying to my mother.

I like gory movies. I like the *Nightmare on Elm Street* stuff, *Friday the 13th*, *Shocker* . . . They're not real, but I think it would be pretty fun to be in one of those things in real life. Like, to be at some camp somewhere and have this guy chasing you around with a chain saw trying to chop you in little pieces. I'd try to kill him first, you know; I wouldn't run away.

That's why I wanna go into the army—the Green Berets or something. I'd love to go into combat. I'd love to just hold a big machine gun and shoot it all over the place.

*What do you want to shoot at, bottles or people?*

People. That's why war would be fun. I mean, you're supposed to do it; it's your job. You don't get into trouble for it. Like, you can't just go over to somebody on the street and blow him away, but in the army you can kill as many as you want. It'd be more fun to shoot at people than bottles. *(With a frightening gleam)* I mean, if you shoot a bottle it just breaks; if you shoot a person then it bleeds and everything.

*If you shot someone and watched him die, bleeding all over the place, don't you think that would bother you?*

No. It doesn't bother a lot of people. Like, Charles Manson—it didn't bother him. He knew what he was doing. I'm not bothered by Charles Manson; I'd bail him out if I had the money. He'd probably kill me though, 'cause he probably doesn't want to get out. There's a lot of people who want to kill *him* because he killed their friends and stuff. But I'd like to talk to him, see what he's like, ask him why he killed all those people.

I've got this book at home about all these people who were buried alive. It's a true story. All these kids were in a bus and these three guys came on and told them to take off their clothes, and they buried them alive.

I was watching "Geraldo" the other day and this guy was on, talking about how he took his girlfriend and chopped her up and boiled her in his room. He was like, "No, the smell didn't really bother me at all." *(Laughs.)* There's a lot of good stuff on TV. I like hearing about killers and what they did and why, and the pictures and everything: "(Rescue) 911," "Unsolved Mysteries," "Cops," "America's Most Wanted" . . .

*Do you ever think they might end up profiling you on that show?*

*(Laughs.)* No. I'm not a psycho. I just like them.

*Why don't you become a cop?*

No, that's not what I like. They just take orders and follow the law and stuff. I want to be independent. Well, when I talked about the army I was really talking about war. The army's just taking orders too, but I wouldn't do that. I'd be there for the war, the shooting. I'd just kill people when I wanted to. Cops can't do that. If they told me I couldn't do something, I'd just do it anyway. If they got in the way, I'd shoot them too—I'd be there for the shooting. Free machine gun, bullets . . . that's what I meant by the army.

*What people do you look up to?*

I like people who don't take any crap from other people, people who do it their own way. I like Donald Trump. He's got all that money, and he's young, and he does whatever he wants to.

*A lot of boys at St. Joseph's talked about guns and hunting; Connecticut produces a lot of sportsmen. Branford, 13, was an ardent hunter and gun enthusiast, already a National Rifle Association supporter. He also looked the part of the hunter, with his square jaw and blond cowlick:*

My family's real into sports. We got a little boat; we go water-skiing a lot. We do a lot of huntin' and fishin'. My dad and me hunt a lot of ducks, geese.

I've been shootin' guns since I was two. I'm pretty good with 'em. Every now and then my dad and me go practice at this club, but we go huntin' enough so we don't really need practice.

I've only gone deer huntin' four times, and I only saw one deer, but it was too far away. I don't think I'd feel guilty about shootin' a deer. Maybe a little bit if it was a female—'cause she might have kids—but not with a male.

*There's a lot of people who think hunting's terrible.*

Yeah, we even had a debate on it in school: guns and hunting. I believe that everybody has the right to own a gun—if they got the permits and everything. I mean, I've always been around guns. When I was a baby I had in my crib a toy gun and these little cardboard decoys. Since then I've always wanted to shoot and hunt. Right now I've got three shotguns of my own.

I don't hunt for the killing. I don't kill an animal unless I'm gonna eat it. I don't think it's right that people go out and kill deer just for fun. It might be fun, but it's not right. I guess the thing I like most about hunting is sitting and waiting for the ducks to come, and then when you start shooting—the shooting is the most exciting part.

I took the NRA course on gun safety. I already knew all that stuff because by dad taught it to me. I think everybody has the right to buy a handgun—it's not guns that kill people, it's people that kill people—and I think assault rifles are OK too, but I understand why other people argue about it. I know you don't need an assault rifle to shoot geese, but I've been to ranges with my dad and some of his friends who brought assault rifles to mess around with, and it was a lot of fun. Why shouldn't you be allowed to bring those on the range? But people should be allowed to buy handguns—you've got the right to protect yourself. There are a lot of stupid people out there who leave their guns around in front of the children, who start shootin' at whoever comes through the door; these people don't know how to take care of themselves or their children.

*Branford impressed me. He presented the NRA argument lucidly and objectively—he was more convincing than many of the adults I have listened to in the past.*

*I was told that, though some kids come to St. Joseph's for religious reasons, most come either for the better education or simply to avoid public school. Benny, nine, was there for religious reasons. This was an odd kid: evasive, nervous, confused, universally disliked by his classmates. He seemed not all there. He behaved as if under the influence of tranquilizers. He was also upset because earlier that morning he was given a violation for playing too close to the statue of Mary:*

I'm gonna be a good-news-spreader when I grow up; I'm gonna spread the good news. I'll be a servant of God and spread the news to poor people. I'll say, "God's alive!" I'll be out there spreading the word to people myself, not just standing on some corner saying, "Go to church. You should go to church."

My family goes to church a lot. I learn a lot about the Bible. Jesus heals the sick man, Jesus heals the deaf man—those are my favorite stories from the Bible. It shows you how good He was.

I think everyone has to worship God. You can't live with God; you can't survive. Even the dinosaurs couldn't live without God. He gives us water and soil, so we can plant our food in it. He helps us when we need Him. If you have a bad problem and you pray to God, He'll help you—you don't even have to be in church—He can always hear you.

But you have to be good to Him too. You can't lie; you can't sin; you have to go to church; you go to a Catholic school; you pray to Him every night. I'm going to make Him happy by helping the poor, giving Bibles to the poor, and spreading the word.

*(Benny slows his speech, making it difficult to follow his sentences from start to finish. This and his wavering tone make him sound like a record being played at the wrong speed.)*

The kids here don't like my ideas. I'll say, "Hey, let's go on top of the monkey bars," and they'll say, "No, we don't like that idea."

They don't like the way I draw either; I did a finger painting today, and they all said it looked like a two-year-old's. They ignore me too; if I do something nice they just don't say anything.

But they're my friends—the only friends I have. I don't have any in my neighborhood because . . . when we moved in, the real-estate guy said, "There's a lot of kids; there are kids all over the place." But they were all babies and stuff, so I don't have any friends in the neighborhood. I can't even ride my bike out of the neighborhood because there's a big hill and I wouldn't be able to get back up.

But my friends don't like me sometimes. Sometimes I pray that Adam won't get on the van, the Kinder-Care van. He's too wild. I never feel good. I get nervous—and I don't like it when he comes on the van because he's wild and noisy! So I prayed and it worked; sometimes he doesn't get on the van.

*What happens if you don't worship God, don't go to church?*

God'll say, "Go! I don't remember you. Get out of my face! I don't want you here! Get out of my kingdom!" And then he'll send you to the place no one wants to go, to the devil. And that won't be fun.

*What happens to kids who don't believe in God?*

They take drugs; they do robberies; they go crazy—they have to be crazy to not believe in God. You have to be crazy to wanna burn in hell. I think some of my friends'll burn if they don't start doing good things. They'll deserve it too.

*Robin, 11, was less enthusiastic regarding ritual. She stated her case against organized religion as clearly as Branford supported the NRA:*

It's a little weird that I'm here in a Catholic school, because I'm not really religious at all. We have a religion class here we have to go to. I just kind of go along with it. My parents think going to church is stupid. I do too. I believe that God exists, but I don't feel like I have to go into a building and praise and sing for a couple of hours every Sunday, the way most people do. And I don't think other people should say you have to, or that you're a sinner if you don't or whatever. I mean, it's hard to believe God knew this was gonna happen—that we should be singing to him and stuff—so why should people say we *have* to do it? You shouldn't do something for God because you *have* to. I don't think God wanted it that way.

*The kids had funny, provocative, and tragic things to say about family and relationships. Gabby was in a strange position: This seven-year-old, a girl no larger than the head of a pin, spent five days a week in the school where her father was principal:*

*What's it like to be the principal's daughter?*

Some of my friends say, I'm gonna tell your dad! I'm gonna tell your dad!" But they never do. A while ago I got a violation—I pushed a boy, and he started crying and had to go to the nurse because he hurt his back on the blackboard—and my teacher told me I had to go to the principal's office. My dad wasn't really angry, though. He just gave me kind of a pep talk.

One time my teacher told me to go out in the hall. I was standing there, and then I saw my dad come walking down the hall. I tried to look the other way, and then I heard, "What happened? What did you do now?" I said, "Dad, please go away, now! This is *school*!"

My dad's nice and stuff, but sometimes it would be better if he wasn't the boss.

*It was spring; birds were chirping, flowers were blooming, and Laura, 11, was in love. Love at the grade-school level is fascinating. There are few kisses and fewer phone calls. Boys and girls often communicate their love through mediators, and the relationship runs its course without the two ever meeting face to face.*

There's a boy that I really like. *(She whispers his name.)* You can't tell him. He's right in the next room. I really like him. I think about him all the time.

*Should I go next door and tell him you'd like to talk to him?*

*Nooooo! Nooooo!* Don't you dare! He knows that I like him; one of my friends told him I liked him at lunch the other day, and he told her that he likes me too. My girlfriends call him up and ask him who, and he says, "I like a girl with two *a*'s in her first name." That's me.

*How long has this been going on?*

All year. Nine months. . . Yeah, I know, it's a long time, and I haven't even talked to him yet—not alone. I talk to him when we're in a group of people. But it's embarrassing. I probably won't get the courage to talk to him until I'm 30.

*And then he'll be bald. Do you like bald men?*

Not really. My father's bald and I like him, but that's different. But *he* won't get bald. He's an athlete.

I think about him all day long. I think about us going places and stuff, and talking to each other at lunch. But that's the way it is. We really are boyfriend and girlfriend now—everybody knows we like each other. But when you get to be boyfriend and girlfriend, you don't really do anything; you just say you're going out. There are two types of going out—that's what everybody says: There's going out, and there's going out out. Going out is like me and him, and going out out is like, when you actually go out. I think going out is better.

*It's really very complicated. Maybe we should just call him in here and see if he can explain it any better.*

If you do, I swear, I'll clobber you.

*Ralph, 12, was one of the few kids I met who spoke so affectionately of a sibling:*

The most exciting thing I've ever experienced is when my little sister was born, last year. It was a surprise in the first place, because my parents didn't plan on having any more kids, so I thought I wouldn't have any brothers or sisters. It was really exciting when it came down to the time when she was, you know, supposed to do it. My sister came at about six in the morning, when I was sleeping at my grandparents' house, but I went to go see her after school that day. I looked at her through the window. It's a real strange feeling to look at your sister for the first time. I'll never forget it.

*More common were kids like Mia, 11, who would gladly swap her siblings for a new pair of shoes. Brothers and sisters can scream and scratch at each other during lunch, resolve the problem, and begin a fresh conflict by dinner. The cycle does them little harm; it's the parents who really suffer:*

I've got two brothers, 15 and 8. We hate each other. Each of us hates the other two. I think it bothers my father the most. He flips out when we start screaming or fighting or whatever. We can't help it; we hate each other *sooo* much. We never get along. Not for a second. At supper, every night, there's a big fight. Last week I threw a plate of spaghetti at my big brother, and he threw his Coke back at me. Dad had a fit.

We drove to upstate New York a few months ago. I didn't think we'd get there alive. My brothers and me were arguing the whole way, and my father screamed at us the whole way. Everybody was pulling everybody else's hair and everything. I think it all started because I didn't want to sit in the middle.

*Talia, 12, was involved in a more substantial conflict. Like so many other kids with foster parents or stepparents, she disapproved of the situation and angrily refused to accept it:*

*You look exhausted.*

You just pulled me out of history class. Thanks.

*(After a minute, she changes the subject to her stepfather. She cringes and grimaces and nearly fogs up her thick, tinted glasses.)*

I have a stepfather. My stepdad's been living with us for about a year and a half. We don't talk much. I don't really like him. I just kind of ignore him. He's just so annoying—everything he does is annoying. He tries to tell me and my sister what to do, and we just don't do it. We try, for my mom's sake, but it doesn't work. My mom's really the man of the house.

He really gets us angry when he orders us to do something. Last week he told my sister, "Close the door!" We just looked at each other and walked away. We don't mind closing the door if he asks us politely, but not if he orders us like a general. A stepfather doesn't have that . . . authority. We don't have to deal with it that much though, because he's always at work. We don't eat dinner together or anything. When he gets home my sister and I are in our rooms.

He's just such a dork, you know. His idea of fun is going to the track and watching all the cars drive around—around and around—and then talking about it all the way home.

*How would you change your family if you could?*

Well, my mom loves my stepfather, so I wouldn't get rid of him, as long as he keeps my mom happy. I guess I'd just make him smarter, and less annoying.

*Candice, 14, was my last interview. She was pretty; tall and slender with smooth, even features. She had a lightness about her, and when she smiled, or shifted in her seat, she did so with the casual grace of a runway model.*

*It was Candice's last day of school for the year, and she was bursting with energy and good cheer. Perhaps that's why she spoke so openly of such private things:*

My sister's a big problem. She's only 15, but she messed up the family a lot. It's weird 'cause, like, except for her the family's normal. My mom and dad aren't divorced like everybody else; we get along real well. She's got these weird friends. They're all older than she is; some of them are out of school. They all have long hair; she's never gone out with a guy with short hair. It's all heavy-metal guys, and that's what my mom doesn't like. They're real scumbags. She got caught up in the whole heavy-metal thing—she just can't stay out of trouble.

She ran away last year—she was 14—with her boyfriend. Her boyfriend was 18. They met at a party or something. My mom wouldn't let her go out with him, but she did anyway, and she kept coming back drunk. She'd bring him back and he'd stay real late. One night she came back at four in the morning and my parents—it was like, the last straw—they told her she couldn't see him anymore. *(Laughs.)* The next night she said she was taking out the garbage and she didn't come back at all. My dad called the police, and when they found her she was in bed with the guy. The policeman told my dad it was his fault because they had let him stay at our house—in my sister's room—until two or three in the morning. He said it was leading him on. But anyway, they put him in jail because she was a minor.

*(I'm taken by surprise—I wasn't expecting such a beautiful mouth to tell such an ugly story.)*

Last summer, my parents came downstairs real late—three or four in the morning—and found some guy having sex with my sister. Then they found her diary and read all these things she had done, and they really lost it. They sent her off to this psychiatric place for a month.

It's weird—I get along with my sister and I don't—I can't explain it. I'm not like her. She's a real rebel. But our rooms are downstairs, right next to each other, so we're always together. *(Laughs.)* Sometimes she gets jealous when her boyfriends come over and they talk more to me than they talk to her.

I'm used to her. I use all these things she does for blackmail. If she comes back drunk or with a guy, or with a guy and drunk *(laughs)*, I say, "I'm gonna wear your black sweater tonight," and if she says no, I threaten to tell Mom and Dad.

I found out she had been using drugs, and I blackmailed her for that. Her old boyfriend was addicted to drugs—he's not now—and he still calls her. When she's not home he tells me all about the things she does. He said she was smoking pot; he said the only reason her new boyfriend goes out with her is because he can, like, use her when he wants to.

My mom put her on birth-control pills. She said, "You're too young for this." But she did it anyway because she had to.

*Do you think there's anything wrong with the way your sister lives?*

Well, I don't know. Maybe not. She goes to public school and I go to Catholic school; can you imagine my sister in this place? *I'm* like a rebel in this place, only because everybody else is real goody-goody. Sometimes, my girlfriend comes over to my house on the weekend and we drink a little. We just drink a little Peachtree schnapps from my parents' liquor cabinet, not enough to get drunk. I guess I didn't answer your question. I don't know . . . I don't know if there's anything *wrong* with the way my sister lives. But for me, I don't want to sleep with a lot of 18-year-old heavy-metal guitar players.

I don't really care. I care more about my friends and my parents—I'm not too close to my sister. If she keeps going and gets killed . . . I'd care about it when it happened, but right now I don't really care.

*Your sister's the messed-up girl in the room next to yours.*

Yes. Exactly. That's exactly it. We don't have too much to do with each other. I go to the movies with my friends; she sleeps with every guy she meets on the street. I know it's mean, but I don't count her as my sister anymore.

I mean, she started destroying the family. Things are OK now, but last year my parents were getting into fights all the time; there was always screaming in the house . . . it was just falling apart. I was thinking, "My sister's gonna get put away; my parents are gonna get a divorce. What's gonna happen to me?" They'd start fighting, the three of them, and I'd just go outside and take a walk, or go into my room and put loud music on. It was embarrassing too, 'cause everyone on the street knew about it. They knew everything, and that was hard on my parents, everyone saying, "That girl's no good. That girl's a slut." We have a politician living on our street, a lot of rich people—it destroyed our reputation.

*(She looks up at me for a few seconds, then smiles and holds my eyes for another moment. She isn't embarrassed. I don't know what to make of it. Perhaps she's just being graceful.)*

After she ran away we started going to this clinic. My mom and dad still go there. I remember one time my dad and my sister were just screaming at each other. My sister was screaming, "Hit me! Hit me!" and I was going crazy, screaming, "Stop it! Stop it!"

My sister was, you know, put away there—that's where she stayed for a month—but my parents and I had to drive for an hour and half *every day* for these family counseling sessions.

She's better now, more under control, but she still comes back drunk a lot. But actually, in the last few days she's been different. You know how you can tell when a person is doing drugs, when their personality changes—that's the way she's been. This morning she was like, "Where's my brush?" I told her I didn't know, and she just started smacking me, and we got into this huge fight over nothing.

And she's still got the whole heavy-metal thing, too. She sits in her room in the dark, head banging. Her room is covered with posters of Guns 'n' Roses, L.A. Guns, Scorpions, Motley Crue. I think that's a bad influence on her. "Kill your mother, kill your father. . . ." That can't help her any.

If it happens again I think my father's gonna sign these papers to put her in residential. He was gonna do that before, but once you do it you can never see the person again, and my mom couldn't handle that. My mom's still, like, in the middle of it; I think my dad's just given up. He's not gonna take anymore of it. That's, like, the difference between mothers and fathers; the father gets to the point where he's not gonna take anymore; the mother's like, "Oh, that's my little girl."

I guess my parents had something to do with the whole thing. They're very strict. If you come back a minute after the curfew, you're in big trouble. I never like that, but I could deal with it; my sister just couldn't deal with it. And when she started going really crazy, my parents gave her—they let her go out; they let people come over late at night. But it didn't help. Maybe it was too late.

*How do you think the whole thing has changed you?*

Well, I guess I have more of an attitude. I know I can get away with a lot more. *(Laughs.)*

*What a depressing story. What bothered me most was Candice's casualness, her cool acceptance of such an extreme situation. Whatever happened to the days when little sisters told on their older sisters for borrowing a sweater without permission? The* idea *of a 14-year-old girl blackmailing her sister by threatening to tell her parents the sister came back at four in the morning, drunk, with a guy—to borrow a sweater! Borrowing without permission isn't nice, but it's more desirable than blackmail.*

*I can't imagine how difficult it must be to raise children. Even model parents have no guarantee that their child will make it through unscathed. I've spoken at length about how difficult it is to be a child in today's America. In an atmosphere where kids are exposed to so many dangers and pressures—drugs, gangs, sex—it's clearly no easier to be a good parent.*

# 9

# Andover, Massachusetts

*By the time I left Bristol I had become so accustomed to being in other people's homes that I reverted to my own at-home behavior and neglected to clean up after myself. I left my friend Cliff's guest room in a chaotic state. To make matters worse, Cliff's wife walked into the kitchen on the morning of my last day there and found me, puffy-eyed, drinking directly from her half-gallon of low-fat milk. It didn't concern me at the time. It was only two months later, at the end of my trip, that I snapped out of the travel groove, saw these offenses for what they were, and apologized in the course of 14 phone calls.*

*At any rate, I drove from Bristol to Boston, where another couch and another cat awaited me. Boston is a beautiful place and, I've always believed, an ideal place to start a family. It has everything. The city is cosmopolitan, with all the benefits of a big city but without the out-of-control growth and grinding pressure of New York or Los Angeles. Massachusetts has its own style; there is no mistaking it for another place. I stayed in Cambridge, by the Charles River, a few minutes from the Harvard campus.*

*Thanks to a relative, I spent an afternoon in Andover (also a beautiful place), about 20 miles north of Boston, interviewing a group of five kids. These kids were all friends and schoolmates. If they hadn't gathered to talk to me, they would still have been together, swimming or malling, so they said.*

*Carolyn, 13, was the newest member of the clan. A year before our interview, she and her family had moved to Andover from Florida. Moving is always a difficult adjustment for kids, even for one as resilient and resourceful as Carolyn:*

I love this place, the change of the seasons and everything, but it's been tough making friends. I think the people were friendlier in Florida. I can remember this girl that moved to Florida the same year I left. After about one week she knew everyone, she had lots of friends. After one week here I hadn't even spoken to anyone. I have this group of friends now, but the other people still aren't sure about me. You know, Boston's a traditional place; I guess the people are like that too; they like to stick to the friends they've always had. That's nice, as long as you've always had friends.

The moving thing is real depressing at first. It's OK now, but in the beginning I came home from school crying a lot. You think about all your friends back home . . . I rang up a pretty good phone bill. I mean, it really hurts—it's real pain. You think that there must be something wrong with you because no one wants to talk to you. You get real lonely, and you think about running away and stuff.

I tried so many things to, like, get in with people, because it seemed like they weren't gonna come to me at all. I'd say hello to someone in the hall and they'd just stare at me. I'd eat lunch by myself. So I started kissing up to people, make a lot of first moves. I'd just go over to people and start talking and hope they didn't call me queer or anything. At lunch, I'd go over to some table and ask if I could sit there. And that was real tough for me because I'm not the kind of person who'll do those things. I even once asked these girls if I could go to the movies with them when I heard them making plans. I'll never do that again,

It's weird. When you sink all the way to the bottom like that, you end up doing things you'd never normally do.

*Denice, 14, also had problems with acceptance and confidence. She was wearing a green-and-white striped soccer jersey that was so large it appeared as though she were zipped inside a sleeping bag. Denice told me her soccer team had a game that afternoon and that she was already afraid she would lose it for them:*

I don't wanna stick out, you know? I try to do what everybody else is doing. I just get the feeling that whenever I stick out, it's in a negative way. *(Laughs.)* Just the other day in social studies I asked a question—nobody asks questions in that class—and everybody laughed at me. I thought it was a good question, but they all thought it was stupid. My teacher said I was 10 minutes late and a dollar short. I don't even know what that means. So, I'm not gonna ask any more questions.

Don't stick out in any way—that's my theory. All my clothes are kind of blah; you won't find any pastels or neons in my closet. I don't say too much—except right now. It's better not to say anything at all than to say something stupid.

Last year we were in Ocean Park, Connecticut, on a school trip. We were going down for breakfast and I wore slippers by accident, instead of putting on my shoes. That was terrible. Everybody cracked up. I ran back and got my sneakers.

I'm the goalie on my soccer team. I'm really not that good, but the coach keeps playing me. I guess nobody else wants to play goalie. When I see that someone is coming towards me, that they're gonna shoot, my heart starts pounding, my throat gets all dry—I'm so afraid of missing an easy save. I stand there through the whole game and just pray that the ball will stay far away from me. That's not what playing sports is all about, is it?

Of course I don't like being like this! I have no fingernails. I throw things around my room. I go crazy when I do something stupid. But that's just the way I am. The only way I can relax is if there's no chance of doing anything stupid. Maybe I should go live in a cave somewhere.

*As I listened to Denice it was obvious that the pressure she felt, the anguish, was genuine—a terrible burden that hung over her and made her older. I never expected to meet so many kids in good circumstances who aroused pathos in me.*

*Randy, 13, was another:*

My dad owns a sheet-metal business with my uncle. Times aren't too good, I guess. He's having problems because a lot of the people he worked for haven't been paying him. They keep putting it off because *they* don't have money.

They worked at this company for 18 years. They bought it about seven years ago. It started going bad a couple of years ago.

They took some kind of loan at the bank and they got 180 days to pay it off, and now it's coming down to it and the money still hasn't come in. I guess they're worried that they're gonna lose the business. They're like, treading water.

He's gotten really quiet. He doesn't talk about it, because he's real nervous about it; he wants to put it out of his mind. His temper's a lot shorter. I feel bad for him, you know, he's got a lot of stress on him. We—my mom and me—try to help him out as much as we can.

I don't take things for granted as much. I know we can't afford to spend as much money as we used to. I mean, my birthday's coming up next week, and I know I can't ask for something that's too expensive. We cut corners. I quit my karate lessons; that was $30 a month. We took the spring-water thing out of the house; that was $30 a month too. I mow lawns. I wrote some applications for jobs last week.

The thing that sucks is, I mean, my father and my uncle haven't done anything wrong. They're just waiting for the money people *owe* them. It seems pretty unfair that you can lose your business because people owe you money.

*I was amazed at Randy's awareness of the crisis his family was facing. I took it as another indication that kids today are more perceptive than previous generations. My family had a similar crisis when I was 13, and it was only years later that I learned the story, and years after that the details.*

*Natalie, 14, also impressed me with her awareness and sensibility. She spoke of divorce and adoption with a coolness I wouldn't even expect her parents to possess:*

My parents are divorced. We live with my mom. My dad picks us up on Wednesday night and takes us out to dinner, and then on Friday we go to spend the weekend here at his place.

Dad left in November. They see each other now and then. I don't know if they'll get back together; maybe they will. Well, I don't know, it's OK as it is. I like spending time with my father, alone, and I like spending time with my mom. Maybe it's better than spending time with them together.

I'm adopted. My mom had a miscarriage in '74 and '75, and so they adopted me. Then they had my brother the next year, and my mom had no problem with it. I can remember when we were really young, my brother would ask my mom, "Mom, did I come out of your stomach?" and she'd say yes. Then I'd ask her, and she'd never answer me.

I found out when I was seven. My mom had these two books that explained it, and she showed 'em to me and stuff. They said why it is kids are adopted, drawings of families together, "Every child is special." Then we talked about it.

When my brother found out, he'd use it every now and then, and that hurt, I guess. Like, if we got into a fight he'd say, "You don't even belong here!" Then I'd smack him. He always knew he could use that, you know. And back then, maybe it made me feel that I really didn't belong. But it doesn't bother me now, and he never says things like that anymore.

Dad said he'd help me find my real parents when I was 18. I'd like to find out. I'd like to know who they are and what they're like. But only once; I just want to meet them once; I don't want to have any long-term relationship with them. I mean, I don't even know anything about them. It's just for curiosity. I wonder if I look like them. That would be kinda weird.

*If you had an adopted child, how would you go about telling her?*

I think my parents did it the right way. I'd just wait until I thought she was old enough to understand, then I'd just tell them. I don't think people should hide it.

But I'm lucky, I ended up with nice parents; I'm sure some

kids aren't as lucky. That's why I want to be a social worker. I'd like to work with kids up for adoption, to make sure they get into good homes.

*Troy, 15, was the odd man in an otherwise professional group of kids. He had long, curly hair shaved to the scalp on the sides, and tiny ears that lay flush against the side of his head, as if they were trying to hide:*

Last year, until we got caught, me and my friends used to walk into Store 24's and steal candy and Cokes and stuff. We all had money; it was just for the excitement, for the "Yeah, I can do it." Then one day we were walking back, and there was this bike sitting by the road, and we took it. We knew the kid from school, and we didn't like him. He told on one of us for skipping class. It was brand new—a real nice bike—and it was just sitting in the kid's front yard. We took it to Brian's house and hid it in this shed they have. Then we stripped it. We were gonna use the parts and the frame.

I guess someone said they saw us or something, 'cause the kid's mother came by and looked in Brian's shed, and then she called the cops. That was a Friday afternoon. We were all over at one of the other guy's house—we were gonna spend the night there—and at about nine the cops came. My heart just dropped. We had to wash police cars for four hours, and we got a record, but it gets erased when we turn 18.

Wow, my mom was pissed off. She yelled for a while. Brian was stupid enough to say, "It's no big deal; it's just a bicycle." He got grounded for a long time.

*These five well-off kids typified the new breed of teenage-adults. They felt anxiety and pressure—all in seemingly adult situations. It occurred to me that kids today suffer from a kind of childhood angst brought on by the same pressures that produced angst in their mothers and fathers and they had an adult awareness of what it was they were feeling.*

*Back in Cambridge I talked to Andrew, 15, whose parents I met by chance. He talked about his father. I won't describe Andrew or the circumstances behind my meeting his parents—the things he said were not very flattering to the father.*

*He peered from underneath the brim of a Boston Red Sox cap, his shifty eyes darting in every direction but mine:*

Don't get me wrong. I love my father and everything, but I think he makes a lot of stupid decisions—a lot of wrong ones anyway. I mean, I'm 15, and sometimes I think I can handle myself better than he can. We fight sometimes, because I can see that he's about to make a mistake—a mistake that affects me—and I don't wanna have anything to do with it. He says, "I know you think you know everything but you're not an adult, and I have to decide what's best for you." What am I supposed to do?

We moved into Cambridge last year when he was offered this job. My mom and I kept saying, "We should stay here for a while until you're settled in there—we lived an hour away—and move when you know everything's gonna work—'cause he has a history of having things *not* work out. But we moved, and one month later he got into a fight with his boss or something and he quit—or he got fired—I'm not sure which.

We've disagreed with each other for a long time. That's why by now I'm tired of it, 'cause I'm the one who ends up paying for it. I remember, I had a chance to go on this great trip with my baseball team, to go play some games in Mexico in this tournament they were having. It was summer! And I was taking this math course because I had some problems with it in school. My father wouldn't let me go on the trip—not for *one* week—because of it. I said, "It's just one week! The course goes all summer! It won't be any problem making the work up—I'll take it with me!" He said no. I didn't say a word to him for like a month. I mean, it was a once-in-a-lifetime opportunity. I was 14 years old. Isn't that what being a kid's all about: seeing things and doing things, getting some experience? He stole that away from me 'cause of some stupid math course that won't ever mean anything to me as long as I pass the course, which I did.

The big thing now is private school. He wants me to go to this prep school because he thinks that's, like, a way of making sure I'll get a good job. These kids in this school don't know what's going on—they're all the kids who go into their father's business and that's it; they never really have to worry about getting out there and doing anything for themselves. That's what I'm gonna have to do, so prep school isn't gonna prep me for anything. I know they got good teachers there and everything, but nothing matters if you never learn how to deal with people—the *real* people. My father doesn't think about that—he's got these ideas of what it's like, but they're just wrong—he doesn't see that things are different from when he was 15. Nowadays, if you can't handle yourself—if you don't know what's going on—you're not worth much. The education in public school may not be *as* good as private school, but it's the real world: You learn how to handle all different things and all different kinds of people. Whenever I try to explain it to my father he just ignores it.

*(Andrew is taking a certain satisfaction in this assault on his father. He's enjoying it.)*

The thing is, my father went to college for four years and studied English lit or something completely useless in the real world. He's got a college degree, but it hasn't done him any good—it's hurt him is all. He changes careers like, every week. How can I listen to his advice?

It sucks that you can't respect your father sometimes, but . . . I know how he fucked up some of his own life by making stupid decisions, so how can I respect that—how can I, like, trust him? I mean, I don't want him to fuck up *my* life like he did his.

*It wasn't easy to like Andrew. Leaving him, I wondered how his father would describe* him. *I remembered something Charles Wadsworth said: "By the time a man realizes that maybe his father was right, he usually has a son who thinks he's wrong."*

# 10

# New York, New York

*I left Boston and stayed a couple of days in Manhattan at a friend's place in Greenwich Village: a studio apartment, where the span of your arms could always find two walls and where you were never far from Thor, the cat. A beast.*

*New York City is the most exciting city in the world. Growing up in the city is a lesson in itself. It's also a trade-off: New York kids see violence and homelessness and inner-city misery every day; they also live in the center of the art and music worlds, where it is possible to experience everything in the way of culture and to meet whatever kinds of people and travel in whatever circles you desire. For better or worse, a child born in New York is not a child very long.*

*I visited my brother in Queens and subwayed back to Manhattan with him and his broken leg. He had difficulty walking with his crutches. It was hot, too, and the poor guy's hands kept sliding off the crutch handles. No one in the subway car offered to give up a seat; no one even considered it. We finally found two places. Ten seconds later two Latin guys, strung-out and slimy, came in and stood in front of me. They emptied two Glad bags on the floor: 50 tubes of Colgate in one and 50 Mennen Speed Sticks in the other. They set about coercing passengers into buying. People checked to see whether their shoelaces were tied. No one budged.*

*Living in New York City requires stamina. Leonard was a diminutive 13-year-old with tortoiseshell glasses and sloping shoulders:*

I was born here in Manhattan. New York City is a great place, but it's really for older people. I can't go out at all, late, because kids will just come over to you and punch you, for no reason. It's happened to me a few times. I'm scared to wear my hat, because I know someone'll steal it. I go out places with my friends and my parents, but for the most part I stay in one area, 80s and early 90s. I live on 88th and Lexington. I don't go to the Village or anything.

New York is really getting pretty dangerous. In fifth grade I'd stay out past six and I'd never even think about it—in the summer when it was light out. But now I'd never stay out past six. Six is when all the other kids come out and start fights and everything, and there's the homeless. . . . No, it's not the kids from the 80s that cause problems, it's the kids from the projects uptown—Harlem, Spanish Harlem—that come down looking for trouble. Even in the 60s you have to be very careful. You have to be smart about it. If you see them coming you duck into a store or something. I mean, you can't be Rambo or anything—these kids would kill Rambo; they're more heavily armed. *(Laughs.)* I ran into a hardware store once when some kids were messing with me, and the guy said, "That's all right, just stay here. I'll protect you." I guess they're used to it, like we are. You have to know, if you have a day off from school, not to go into Central Park if public schools are off too, because they'll all be out there. Two weeks ago my friend and I were walking on 90th and York, and we turned the corner and there was a group of about ten Spanish kids coming the other way. We ran into a deli, but they came in after us. One of them said to me, "Hey, I like your hat. Can I try it?" I told him he couldn't because it was new, and they backed off. Right as we got out of the deli one of them just took it right off my head.

Last year I was walking with my friend right in our own neighborhood, and we didn't notice there was a group of black kids behind us. They stopped us and asked for our coats. We tried to run—it was on the side street one block from my house—but they caught my friend and punched him in the mouth.

*Why do these kids leave their neighborhood for yours?*

Because a lot of them think, "Let's go get the rich kids." They think everybody that lives below 90th is rich, every white kid is rich. So they come for us because they know they can beat us up, and they know they can steal stuff: jackets, hats, gloves. I think most of them do it for the fun.

Private schools around here have security, because sometimes the Latin kids will just stand outside and wait for the kids to get out.

*(A strange thing about New Yorkers: They abhor the violence in their city, and recognize that it affects their lifestyles, yet they all exalt the craft of surviving these dangers. Leonard is no exception.)*

You get to know where you're safest. Fifth Avenue is pretty good until 96th; Park Avenue is OK until the subways come up; Lexington is bad after 93rd; Third is the same. It's weird—you walk up Park Avenue and it's all nice buildings and stuff, then all of a sudden you're in trouble. It can change completely in just one block. And everybody knows it; they know exactly where it changes. That's how you survive.

You have to be careful. When my mother was pregnant with me she was mugged in Central Park by a guy with a gun. It was in the middle of the afternoon, and she didn't think anyone would bother a pregnant woman in broad daylight. My dad's cousin came for a visit a while ago, and he was like, "How can you deal with this? You must have to put blinders on your eyes not to see all this." I guess we do have blinders on. We walk by the homeless, we don't give people money because we know they'll buy drugs with it.

*What do you do to have fun and be safe at the same time?*

We go to the movies or we hang out in pizza places and talk. . . . Yeah, it is a shame—I live in the most exciting city in the world, the city that doesn't sleep, but all I do on the weekends is go to the movies and eat pizza. But that'll change when I get a little older and bigger, when I can go wherever I want to.

Me and my friend watched "The Wonder Years" a couple of weeks ago and we both thought, "Wouldn't it be great to live in that time? We could stay out late as we wanted to; there's no danger; they all live in real *houses* with back yards and everything." But at the same time we know this is a special place. It would be strange to have to ask for a ride somewhere, instead of just getting a cab. Everything that exists in the world, you can find here. I like New York, but I'd like to live somewhere else eventually. I'd like to have a yard and a dog and a swimming pool. A nice suburb somewhere. That's what I'd like for *my* kids. But I don't know . . . people always tell me, "Born a New Yorker, always a New Yorker."

*What would you do if you were mayor of this city?*

I'd clean up the uptown area. I'd clear out all those vacated buildings. After that, the people would be more decent, not as much drugs and everything. I'd build more jails and get the death penalty going.

*Ally was a prodigy far beyond her 12 years—an accomplished, classically trained violinist. Only in New York City can you find a 12-year-old this hip:*

People who spend all their time worrying about things really annoy me. What a waste of time. There's so much happening, so much to see, but so many people are too busy screaming at taxi drivers and stuff. I don't worry about getting mugged—not until I actually see someone coming up to me. That's when it's time to worry, not before.

I always think the people in this city are just like the buildings. Half of them are really special, the other half should be destroyed. Then there are some that look good on the outside but are really nothing on the inside.

*As I had anticipated, New York proved the most difficult place to gain permission for interviews. There were only Leonard and Ally (the result of a family friend's effort) and the following two, arranged by a friend who worked with underprivileged kids.*

*I met several kids like Manuel and Damon when I worked with runaways, and for me these interviews were routine. In the context of the wide range of experiences of the kids interviewed for this book, however, I recognize they may be something of a shock. I left their language and the expression of their hostility intact, rough as it is, because, very simply, it is the common language of inner-city ghetto kids.*

Manuel, 12, was wearing a denim, sleeveless vest and fingerless gloves. He talked about sex for the duration of our half-hour, and he was aiming to impress:

There's lotsa bitches my age havin' sex—they like it even if they say they don't. I got it for the first time last year by 'dis bitch was 14. *Maaaannn*, she was good. I knew what I was doin' n' shit, but I was a little scared, 'cause she was older and she 'ad dees tits n' shit. Man, she musta fucked a lotta guys, 'cause she knew what she was doin', and she knew how d' do it *good*! That bitch was blowin' me'n' shit—I'm lucky I didn't catch nothin'. I got one a my friends caught some shit from some bitch—fuckin' crabs, man. They wuz all over d' place—all over 'is bed and 'is clothes n' shit. He went back and fucked 'er up, man, n' she deserved it. But anyway, 'at was one a the greatest things ever happened d' me.

I had a lotta girls after that, you know. I mean, I'm pretty popular n' shit, and d' chicks know they'll be doin' good for themselves if they hang w' me. They all fuck, too, you know, 'cause if they don't, ain't no boys'll talk to 'em. It's good, you know, 'cause they start when they's 10 or 11, so they get real good when they're 12 or 13. They know the better they are d' more popular they'll be.

*How important do you think girls are?*

Shit man, they're *important*. *(Laughs.)* If you couldn't get laid, whaddya do? But that's why they're important. They got pussies. That's why they're important. Everythin' else is for d' men. It's like

Africa—the old days—where d' man hunts and the girl cooks n' shit. 'At's just d' way it is.

Dats fun too, man, you know, like, havin' some bitch does whatever you says. You go like, "Gimme dat thing over there," and she gives t' ya. You go like, "Blow me," or somethin' n' she does it. Shit man, dats fun!

*That's the inner-city perspective. These kids never even have a childhood; they graduate directly from infant to adult.*

*One very striking trend I noticed in my interviews with these kids was faith in upward mobility. From small kids to the 15-year-olds, slum kids told me again and again that they would be doctors and lawyers. Many told me they'd work until they got to be like Donald Trump.*

*One such kid was Damon, 14, from Harlem, whose sneakers and socks were riddled with holes.*

I wanna be a big-time lawyer, like that black guy on "L.A. Law," wi' dat clothes and 'at fancy-talkin' shit, you know? Work in the office, drive home in some sports car, fuck d' old lady—some nasty high-class bitch—'at's what I'm gonna do.

I'm gonna get outta here, you know. I'll graduate from high school and I'll go to college somewhere. I know that's important. I play hoops, you know, so maybe I'll get a scholarship or somethin'; and den I'll get to be a lawyer, or maybe a doctor. But I like bein' a lawyer 'cause den I'd save some a the black people in jail for shit they didn't do. Black people need black people to help 'em out 'cause the whites don't give a fuck about niggers from Harlem n' shit, you know?

*Slum kids don't often become professionals, getting out of the slum is hard enough. These kids have to fight for everything: food, safety, shelter, parents. They must know this; their whole existence is based on an awareness of the harsh realities. Why do they believe they'll end up living the soap-opera life that so appeals to them? Perhaps it's self-deception, an illusion, an oasis of freedom in an otherwise desolate world of submission.*

*It's frustrating. I grew up with all the advantages a kid needs to make something of himself, and I fought all along. I was a pretty shiftless kid—but for those born under the right circumstances there is always a way; a way into something else; a way out of trouble. For a kid like Damon there is only bondage and drudgery, or crime. During these last two interviews I realized how simple the situation really was: After the interviews, I was free to drive away, to New Jersey and shortly thereafter on to Pittsburgh; Madison, Wisconsin; Minneapolis; Denver; Portland, Oregon; and Los Angeles. Damon and Manuel were not.*

*Ironically, I didn't have an easy time getting out of Manhattan that day. I hit the Lincoln Tunnel at exactly five and reached the other side almost two hours later. That made my escape even sweeter; stuck in the tunnel I lived in a slum, caught up in a daydream of what it must be like to be kept down. When the traffic moved and I made it through the tunnel, I experienced, vicariously, the liberation that ghetto kids dream about. It was, I'm sure, the first time I was ever happy to enter New Jersey.*

# 11

# Tara

*During the rest of June I made stops in Pittsburgh and Madison, Wisconsin, without any result. Being back on the Motel 6–Denny's circuit, always surrounded by empty 7-Eleven coffee cups and scrunched-up Taco Bell burrito wrappers depressed me, and I lost all momentum. So I returned to Minneapolis, for pleasure, and stayed there a week. The lake where I had skated was now filled with ducks and lily pads and surrounded by tanned joggers and roller bladers.*

*I called Dave Pedersen, the man who had given me so much help during my last visit. He had told me three months before that his 16-year-old daughter would make an interesting interview. She had, he said, big problems. She had been in an alcohol treatment center (though he said he didn't think she had an alcohol problem) and had been institutionalized when it appeared she might be some threat to herself. She was confined in this institution when I first met Dave.*

*But now she was home and Dave said she was much better. I went to Dave's house to interview her; she thought it was a great idea. So did her father. Dave said he had begun an active effort to help his daughter with her problems and that he believed an open conversation between us would be therapeutic.*

*Tara was not what I had expected. With the exception of her tired eyes, she looked the picture of health. Tall, thin, long curly blond hair, bright blue eyes—very beautiful. She didn't look like a 16-year-old with problems; she looked like a 25-year-old woman with a responsible position in an accounting firm and a fridge full of fresh vegetables.*

*Like her father, she was frank, energetic, and animated. She seemed happy and was more than willing to tell her story. We sat for a long time:*

*(Laughing)* I've always been kind of high-strung. I've always had a low opinion of myself, since I was just seven or so. That's when my parents got divorced. That was really hard on me, and I was right at that age when those things can hurt you the most. I just couldn't accept it. I thought it was my fault; I thought no one loved me; I thought it was because of me that my parents didn't love each other. I used to sit underneath the kitchen table and rock back and forth saying, "No one loves me. I wish I was dead. I'm a terrible person. I wish I was in my grave." I'd do it all day. My mom would sit there and tell me she *did* love me, but I just didn't believe her. Now that I'm older I know she loved me, but at the time I was thinking, "How could they possibly love me if they just got divorced?" I just couldn't deal with it. I blamed everything on myself. And I guess I kind of carried that with me afterwards.

Anyway, I went off to live with my mom. I saw my dad every other weekend.

Somehow I ended up a real tomboy. I dressed like a boy; my hair was like a boy's. I can remember going into a new school in sixth grade and having everybody say, "What's wrong with that girl? She's trying to be a boy or something." Everyone hated me. They told me I was ugly. Every day I had someone come over to me and say, "God, you're ugly!" I couldn't understand it. I asked my mom if I was ugly, and of course she said I was beautiful. I was so confused. It didn't help my confidence. I thought I was ugly and stupid—and I *knew* that everybody hated me.

Things took a real strange turn when I was 13, when I went into seventh grade, junior high. It was a new school, a lot of new people, and I guess I took the opportunity to get rid of the tomboy thing. I started wearing dresses and I pulled my hair back . . . after all that I got to the point where I said, "OK, Tara, you've got to be a girl now." *(Laughs.)* All of a sudden people liked me. Guys thought I was pretty. People were saying, "Wow, she's really changed." I was like, "Good God, what the hell's going on here?" *(Laughs.)* I started liking people. Everyone liked me. I was just a little popular—I had friends for the first time.

I started hanging out with this one girl, Louise. Then I started really working to get the popular, preppy kids to like me and stuff. I remember one of them coming to me and saying, "What are you doing hanging around that Louise for? She's such a geek." Here I was, the ex-Most Hated Girl in the World, and this . . . I didn't understand it. Then I thought, "Oh, this girl is what I used to be like." The preppy kids didn't want me to hang around with her, so I dumped her. I just ignored her. Just like an After-School Special.

I became, like, a monster. I wanted everyone to like me—it was an obsession. I *needed* to have the most popular kids know who I was. So after the summer I went into the eighth grade with this real funky haircut, really cool, shaved in the back and everything. Everybody was like, "Wow, look at her."

But I still wasn't happy, I still hated myself. I kept doing everything I could to be popular and stuff. I started going to parties in ninth grade. If people were smoking then I smoked; if it was cool to drink a beer then I did it. In tenth grade we partied a lot on the weekends—that's the way it is. We'd go to someone's house and just get smashed.

I wasn't a slut like the other girls. I never really liked boys. I never let them do much. Except for this one time—I can't believe it happened. I was at this party in tenth grade—I was 15—and I was in one of the rooms just kissing this guy, and he started getting real rough and into it and everything. Usually I just tell them to stop and that's it, but this guy just started . . . I didn't know what to do 'cause I knew if I stopped him he might start rumors about me or something. It was kind of like I was raped, but I could have done something to stop it, screamed or whatever. I broke up with him the next day. That messed with me a lot. I don't trust guys now. I think that was my first and last time. Some guy told me I passed out at a party and he, you know . . . *(Tara pulls her long legs onto the sofa, kicks off her shoes, and tests four or five positions until she finds the one most comfortable.)*

So I didn't trust guys; I didn't like myself; school sucked; and I wasn't getting along with my parents. They had all these rules, curfews—they didn't trust me at all. They never even knew I drank, and they still didn't trust me. I was trying to make something out of myself, and that strictness didn't work. I guess I was causing them problems. My dad kept asking me if I was drinking or doing drugs. He got involved in this Life Spring Foundation family thing, where you go on a retreat with other families that have problems, and you just talk about life and things; you learn about communication. I know it sounds a little cheesy, but it wasn't that bad—I just wasn't ready for it. My mom was doing everything she could to make me be like her, and I didn't want that. They were blaming each other for my problems.

It was just as bad at school. Everyone liked me, but I didn't have any real friends—just the people I was acting for. I got real depressed. I started thinking what a shitty person I was; shitty 'cause I drank, shitty 'cause I was doing anything I had to, to be popular. I started skipping school all the time—three or four times a week. I knew these girls that were office runners at school; they were the ones who brought the attendance slips from the teachers to the office. They just marked us as present. And I started shoplifting. Me and some friends would cut school and go into town—into Carson's or The Gap—and we'd steal a lot of clothes. We'd steal candy or lunch. I don't know why we did it; it was just kind of a rebellion. For me it was being cool too; "If they're doing it, I'll do it." Sometimes we'd cut school and go to guys' houses. One time we stayed at this guy's house all afternoon and got real drunk and stayed there all night. It was just a wild party in the middle of the week. And these girls I was with were real sluts; they're with a new guy every night—or every party. So we were all plastered, and the other girls were off screwing the guys. I didn't touch anybody—I haven't touched too many people at all since that first time—but the staying out all night was going pretty far for me. I was just falling to pieces. *(Something in the way Tara is telling her story reminds me of the runaways I've known; a certain control and objectivity, the result of counseling.)*

One day in school I just broke down. I got a C on a test, and I had to go down to the office 'cause I was in some kind of trouble, and I was standing out in the hall and I just started crying. I said to the secretary, "I've gotta go home." She brought me into the counselor's office, and I talked to her for a while. She was like, "There's something more than this, isn't there?" I told her it was just the pressure from school starting to build up. She arranged for me to talk to another counselor. That was about a year ago.

I went to this other lady and talked to her for 30 minutes, and she goes, "Have you ever drank alcohol?"

"Yes."

"Have you ever gotten drunk?"

"Yes."

"Well, tell me about your history. Do you have a history of alcoholism in your family?"

I told her my grandfather was an alcoholic—and that was it! She was like, "Yup, I've got an alcoholic here! I knew it!" She said, "I think we should try you out for this alcoholism program we have." I told her I wasn't an alcoholic—that I drank at parties on weekends like very other kid in the world, and she said, "Well, you'll fit in there anyway because you have low self-esteem. So do alcoholics." So I went. I know—I knew then—that I had that problem, a low opinion of myself. So I went.

I went to the program at District Memorial Hospital for a total of eight days. On the first day, we were at this meeting, and they asked me, "How long have you been an alcoholic?" I said, "I'm not an alcoholic. I'm in here for other reasons." They were like *(she imitates their condescending tone)*, "We know. We understand. But you know, accepting you've got an alcohol problem is the first step." They were talking to me like I was five! "No. *You* don't understand. I'm not an alcoholic. I'm in here for something else." I tried and I tried—I just couldn't get anywhere with them. Oh, God, that pissed me off. That's when I started losing it. I mean, I knew I had some problems, and I didn't mind getting help for them, but I didn't have an alcohol problem! I hated myself, and I was doing stupid things because of it. That was the problem. But I had to go to AA meetings and chemical dependency classes with alcoholics and cocaine addicts. Yeah, that's just what we did; all sitting around in a circle, and the instructor says, "Tara, why don't you introduce yourself." I didn't know what was going on, and the guy next to me says, "Just say, 'Hi, my name is Tara, and I'm chemically dependent.' " So that's just what I did. You just go with it. Unbelievable.

I called my dad after a couple of days. I don't know why. I said, "Dad, I just want you to know that I'm in here because I drank and I cut school and I shoplifted. And he said, "So, Tara, you're a thief. And you're a liar." I think that was the worst thing that ever happened to me. I couldn't stop crying—that stupid kind of crying where you can't finish a word or a sentence. I was hoping I could, like, open things up, clear things up by being honest with him, and he called me a liar. I told him to go to hell—never curse in front of my father—and I hung up. I swear to God, you've never, never, seen anybody cry like that. I was shaking and convulsing and everything.

A couple days later my mom and dad came to take me out to dinner. My dad—I'll never forget this—he walked over and tried to, like, make me hug him. That's something—I'm not an affectionate person. Period. I don't want to be touched. If you want to be affectionate to me, verbalize it; and after that phone call. . . . He said, "Come on Tara, give me a hug." I told him I didn't ever want to hug him, and he started, like, trying to force me to hug him. I yelled something. *(Laughs.)* I told him I was gonna call 911. I ran to my mom and said, "Mom, dad's trying to make me hug him!" Pretty silly. My mom was telling my dad that it was his fault I was screwed up, that I was in the alcohol place; it was because of the Life Spring Foundation stuff he was into. I told her it wasn't—it was half *her* fault I was there. She was the one trying to control me.

I just started falling apart after that. I was so depressed and frustrated. I just broke down at one of these meetings and started crying. And that was all they needed.

After the eight days they told me they were sending me to Riverwood, this place in Wisconsin for lunatics, the serious problems like suicide—there was a lot of kids with bandages on their wrists—and severe depression and just plain mental cases. My mom was gonna pick me up at the alcohol place and drive me to Riverwood.

I couldn't believe it. I almost lost my mind in those eight days and now this. All I needed was some serious counseling, someone to help me so I wouldn't be so tense, or feel a little better about myself. I didn't deserve to be shipped off to the nut house. I was sitting outside waiting for my mother, and I was thinking about running away. I was looking down the street and making a plan, but it was already dark outside, and I didn't have any money, and I had nowhere to go. And then my mother drove up and took me to Wisconsin.

*(Tara's mouth falls open, and she shakes her head slowly from side to side, as if in disbelief. She loses some of her control and becomes emotional.)*

Oh God. Oh my God, that was a nightmare. Everything was locked; locked doors all over the place. I was in this, like, reception place, and they took everything away from me. They were nasty people, too. They took my hairspray, anything with alcohol in it; they took my razor and anything sharp; they took clothes they said were "revealing" and a pair of shorts they said were too short, my biking shorts. I was like, "You can't do this! These are my things!" I wanted to scream. Yeah, right, it's bad enough being in Wisconsin.

There I am, walking down the corridor with my mother, and all the other kids are like, "Oh, look at the new girl." Guys were whistling. Body search. Then I get into my white room, all alone, turned out the light and tried to sleep. Not a minute, not a single minute. I couldn't believe I was in there to be *helped*. I've never felt worse.

I mean, I had been in that alcohol place for eight days listening to people talk about my problems; now they were doing it with locks on all the doors. I started thinking that I had more problems than I even knew about—I was just losing my mind. I can't describe it. I felt like I was gonna explode. "If this is life, I just want to die." I was thinking how nice it would be if I could just lie down and die. It's a good thing they took my razor, 'cause after one hour in there I decided, "This is the lowest I've ever been. I hate my life. It's never gonna get better. I just want to die." I kept thinking about different ways I could kill myself.

The next day they put me in the program. They had different levels: level one, two, three. Level one has no privileges, and that's just what I was. Level two, you get to go outside when you're with an instructor. Level three, you get to go out by yourself for 15 minutes at a time, and then longer. I was a level one for two weeks; I couldn't go outside for two weeks. I was like, "This is insane. I gotta get out of this place."

They controlled you in that place—or they tried to—and that's what really sucked. Everyone hated that. All the kids did everything they could to piss off the staff. If they told you to do something you told them to fuck off. If they told you you couldn't do something you told them to fuck off.

The girl who had the room next to me, Martha, was really wild, rebellious. After I was there about a month, we decided we were gonna run away. We called this guy Ron, who had gotten out a week or so before, and we arranged for him to pick us up. So me and Martha and this guy Mitch ran away. Mitch broke down this one door that was locked; it really wasn't too hard to get out.

We ran to the Dairy Queen where Ron was supposed to be but wasn't. Five minutes later two of the instructors from Riverwood drive up. But they couldn't do anything! If you're off their property they can't touch you. They told us to get in the car with them, and Mitch—he's a guy that's been through it all, a guy who *belongs* in Riverwood—tells them to fuck off. He starts walking towards the bridge; Riverwood was right on the Wisconsin-Minnesota border, and the bridge went right to Minnesota. We followed him. They yelled that they were calling the police and we started running.

When we got to the other side of the bridge, Ron drove up, and we drove to Minneapolis. We went out to dinner—Ron had a lot of money on him—and we got a motel room and we went swimming. It was so good to be out.

I called my mom from the motel to tell her that I was OK, and she said she'd come and pick me up. It was already midnight, and we paid for the room, so I told her I'd stay there and go back to Riverwood the next morning. We argued, but eventually she realized that I wasn't going to come home that night, so she made me promise to call Riverwood and tell them I'd be back in the morning. That took like half an hour. She wasn't too happy about me staying there.

I wish I hadn't stayed there. Ron started coming on to me, so I got Mitch to take me out to get some stuff for my contact lenses; they were all dried up. When we came back, Martha was gone. Ron was pretending to sleep, of course. We asked him where she was. I was freaking out. He said, "I don't know what happened to her. I was sleeping." I thought someone had come in and taken her. I looked all over for her.

The next morning we went back. We got two days' restriction where we couldn't leave our rooms. On the third day Martha came back. I sat in her room, and she started crying. She said, "Tara, you can't tell anyone, but I didn't just leave the motel room. I called my mom and she picked me up. Ron raped me." I couldn't believe it. She still had bruises on her wrists where he was holding her down. She wouldn't tell the police or anything, and she made me promise not to. So that was it—you escape from prison, you get raped, and you go back again, and the guy's out having a party.

*(We take a 10-minute break, and Tara makes coffee—one thing is common to most kids who have experienced life on the edge: They drink a lot of coffee. When we sit down again, Tara is all smiles. She's anxious to tell the rest of her story—the happy ending.)*

It's all over now. I was in that place for two months. They didn't want to let me go, but my mom finally signed me out. I settled back in with her, it's been about six months now. It's much better now, I guess because everyone knows that there is, or was, a problem. . . . No, I didn't get anything out of Riverwood. But when I got out I felt great. *(Laughs.)* Really, it was great to be home. I had a positive attitude for the first time in a long time. I can't really explain it; I was free, I was back in control. It was different with my parents from the first day I was back. It was like we had open communications; we were all on the same side. We talk now, the three of us. And I go to this counselor who helps me a lot; my assignment for this week is to write down all the compliments I get. He's helping me to build up my self-esteem. It's still pretty low sometimes, but it's better.

I'm a varsity cheerleader. . . . Yeah, I knew you'd laugh; I don't blame you. I did some cheerleading in junior high school. It's fun; I'm good at it. It's like, when I'm cheerleading, I can hardly believe I was ever in Riverwood. I'm going to cheerleading camp on Monday—I'm so excited! Another big thing is I started working at Taco Bell. I just got my first check—$200; more than I've ever had at one time. I went out and spent it all shopping, buying clothes for cheerleading camp.

All of it makes me feel good. I feel more independent now. Buying clothes is more satisfying than stealing them from Carson's. I don't do any of that stuff anymore.

The only place where I'm still screwed up is with relationships. I just don't want any. Boys just scare me. I never did like them. I never had any relationships. I know if I get to like a boy, he'll dump on me; if I start a relationship, it'll fall apart. I get my attention from cheerleading. I go out with boys, but I never have any kind of relationship. I'm not too big on the whole touching thing, not with anybody.

But I always think about falling in love. It's the greatest thought; you meet someone and you want to be with them all the time. Maybe that'll happen someday, but not soon—I'm only 16 anyway. But I'd like to buy myself some shorter legs first, and bigger breasts; there's still a lot of things about myself I want to change.

*Meeting you now, you don't come off like someone with a self-esteem problem.*

*(Laughing.)* I know. But I am. It's just that I'm pretty tough on the outside, after all this.

*Tara's story reminded me of a few runaway girls I had known, but Tara had a sense of foundation beneath her feet and a supportive family—things foreign to most runaways—and though she wasn't out of the woods yet, she was headed in the right direction.*

*Tara was a very rare type—a kind of woman-child: too emotionally developed to enjoy relaxed innocence; too raw and naive to understand her emotions. She was really very charming. Above all she had the gift that always gets me: the gift of pathos. Perhaps that's why Tara and her story remain so vivid in my memory.*

# 12

# Denver, Colorado

*Moving into the western half of the United States, I discovered I had to adapt to a new way of thinking. I learned this at a Super 8 in Lincoln, Nebraska. It was late when I arrived, and the girl at the desk informed me that there was only one room left and that it had a waterbed. A waterbed? At a budget travel lodge in Lincoln, Nebraska?*

*Inside the room I prodded the bed. There was water there, somewhere, but there was also a standard mattress, all of it under several layers of sheets and contour sheets and blankets. I was exhausted, but I had to get to the bottom of the whole waterbed thing. I peeled off the sheets and found a heavy-plastic inflatable-raft-looking deal filled with water, lying atop the mattress, covering roughly half the surface area of the bed. It was a raft. Or something like it. For this they charged an extra four or five dollars.*

*I ended up taking the raft off the bed, not because it was uncomfortable—I couldn't even feel it—but simply because I felt ridiculous sleeping on a raft on a bed. When I awakened the next morning I was thinking western. I was in the West, the land of cowboys and movie stars and religious gurus.*

*I drove to Denver, following the long arm of Dave Pedersen, who had arranged for me to meet a writer there who would help me find kids. After settling in at the Howard Johnson's Motor Lodge and drinking one of their legendary orange sherbet freezes, I drove to the suburb of Englewood, met my contact, and eventually sat down with Brandy, 15. Englewood is an upper-class suburb, so I was surprised when Brandy, a preppy-looking girl in plaid shorts and Topsiders, spoke to me of gang violence:*

I go to Cherry Creek High School. It's, like, the snobbiest school in Denver. Swimming pool; golf course; kids drive to school in Porsches . . . people I meet hear I go there and they're like, "Ewww." I can't help it; it's a public school. It is pretty preppy; all the guys have Dockers and Topsiders, Polo shirts, cardigans.

But Denver is getting a lot rougher. The whole gang thing is one of the biggest issues in town. The Crips and the Bloods have really set themselves up and, like, recruited the local kids. It's weird because our biggest rival, Thomas Jefferson High in downtown, is all gangs. All their athletes are gang members and everything. You always hear about a shooting in their school or kids caught bringing guns in or whatever. Drive-by shootings in the school parking lot. Everyone always says it's only a matter of time before something big happens at one of the games. They have lots of kids there when they come to play us in something, and they don't like losing—and they *hate* Cherry Creek.

A couple friends of mine were at a Dairy Queen a few weeks ago, by school, and some kids came over from Jefferson. They asked my friends what school they went to, and they said Cherry Creek, and then the guys just started punching them—they really beat them up. They were gang kids that hate rich kids from Cherry Creek. It's also got a lot to do with poor black kids and rich white kids. TJ is mostly black; Cherry Creek is all white. The whole thing is getting rougher. All the different groups in the city and the suburbs are getting at each other's throats; the blacks and the whites, the Hispanics and the whites, the Jews . . . here in *this* neighborhood, a few months ago, a Jewish family had swastikas painted on their house. I think it's all because of the gangs; the whole thing is about violence. It's just weird, you know, 'cause

Englewood is a rich, white suburb. It's weird that all this stuff happens in a place like this.

Drugs are getting more popular. Acid is the most popular drug at Cherry Creek. I tried acid once. It was last year, when I was 14. I was with a girlfriend, and one of her friends gave us some acid. He told me it was only half a hit and it wouldn't do much, but as it turned out it was a full hit and it did a lot. My friend was wearing a fringe jacket, and I was staring at it, and I started hallucinating. I thought it was people hanging off the end of her jacket. The guy who gave me the hit, he held up pictures in front of my face, and they started moving around and talking and everything. I had no grip on myself, you know? I'll never try it again.

*Brandy's classmate, Doris, was less concerned with the escalating violence. Of greater concern to her was the chewing gum she kept in permanent cracking position, between her lower lip and her teeth. When she cracked her gum, every 30 seconds or so, it looked like she was chewing tobacco:*

I'm on the phone all the time. About three hours a night. We have that third-person party thing, so three of us will talk on the phone all night. It's mostly my girlfriends I talk to . . . probably three long calls a night, and maybe one or two short ones. I'll talk to a guy every now and then, but you know how guys are on the phone. . . . Well, they never say more than one word at a time. They're boring to talk to:

"How ya doin'?"

"Fine."

"What's goin' on? What're ya doin'?"

"Nothin'."

"Are you goin' to the party on Friday?"

"Maybe."

That's not my idea of a conversation. If I spent an hour on the phone with a boy I'd end up a vegetable.

*But if you talk to your friends on the phone, after spending the whole day with them at school, how do you come up with enough new material to last the hour? There's only about five hours in between.*

*(Laughs.)* I guess in those five hours we've had time to think about the things we said earlier in the day. But there are also some subjects that you can always talk about: guys, plans, clothes.

We call out of state sometimes and charge it to someone else's credit-card number. If it goes through we talk to California for an hour or so.

*Yeah, but you know, if the guy who owns the credit card looks at his bill and knows that he didn't call California for 60 minutes, he'll call you or the phone company. Your number's on the bill, right between his and the price of the call.*

(Silence.)

*The next day I met Crystal, six, who was on vacation from Ogallala, Nebraska. It was difficult to understand her; throughout the interview she had all four fingers stuffed into her mouth. She refused to take them out:*

My little sister's gonna be turning two next month.

*Do you have to change her diapers?*

Not if they're poopy. Then I don't touch them. But I like to play house with my friend. One of us plays the mother, and the other one plays the daughter. We go shopping and make food and stuff. It's the most fun being the mom, because you tell the others what to do and they obey. I play house with my little sister sometimes, and sometimes I say, "It's time for you to go to sleep." She doesn't always do it, so I keep telling her, and if she still doesn't listen I go play with my dolls.

Sometimes me and my friend play that we're both moms and we both have two kids and we're sisters. We say, "It's time to change their diapers," and we got into different rooms.

When I play house with my friend, we play for about three hours. If it's my sister, it only lasts a few minutes.

*Not a care in the world. My next interview was in the downtown area with a girl 10 years older and not quite as careless. Gabrielle, 16, had a prominent lisp that turned* s's *and* sh's *into* th's. *She was very pretty and stylish, wearing a dark pinstripe blazer and tie as well as the requisite torn Levis. Her first words were, "You don't have to worry about asking me about my lisp. It doesn't embarrass me." So we talked about her lisp and how it affected her:*

Sometimes I get really depressed because of it. When I go somewhere, like on vacation, or when I meet new people, I can see that they're thinking about it. It makes you feel that there's something wrong with you, that you're not normal.

I've thought about it a lot; I'm *not* normal. I can't speak right. I'm never going to be that way. Every time I meet someone—like a guy—the first thing he'll notice is my lisp. It won't be like, "Oh, she's got beautiful eyes," or "Oh, she's really funny"; it'll just be, "Ewww, lithen to the funny way thee talkths."

I don't, like, feel real sorry for myself. I know it's not as bad as being blind or deaf or anything, but it's still there. It's there all the time. You read about blind people who live normally and do everything normal people do. They don't accept it; they try to ignore it. I can't do that. I accept that I'm different and that people will always think I'm different, or stupid. When you talk like me, people automatically assume you're stupid.

We went on vacation last year to the Bahamas. I met some kids there, and we hung out by the pool during the day and walked on the beach. I really liked one of the guys. He was real cute, and it seemed like we were gonna get together. He was from Denver, and I was thinking *(Laughs)*, "Wow, I'll have a boyfriend, and we can meet on the weekends and go to the junior prom and everything, and I could tell my friends that I had a boyfriend I met on the beach in the Bahamas"—how romantic! Anyway, one night we were all on the beach—they had gotten some beers—and one of the other guys started imitating me. He was saying, "Thee thells thea thells down by the thea thore." The boy I liked, he just laughed with them. Needless to say, nothing ever happened.

I was really mad, but like I said, I accept that kind of stuff. It's always going to happen. You just handle it the best you can. I'm sure I'll meet a nice guy someday who doesn't mind. But then—I know this is crazy—he'll have to accept it too, 'cause all his friends will meet me, and then *he'll* be the one who has to start dealing with it, having a girlfriend that speaks funny.

*Different kids—the ones with lisps, the ones 10 inches shorter than the others—often benefit from their differences later in life. They grow up with a special sensitivity and introspection. Unfortunately, it does them little good in the teenage years, where being different is a curse. They suffer. Gabrielle, for all her bravado, was still suffering from the insensitivity of the boy she met on vacation. It's a big price to pay for maturity.*

*Back in Englewood I talked to two baby-sitters. Bettina, 13:*

I sit for my neighbors. They have a seven-year-old girl. I'm with her once or twice a week from, like, 5 to 10. Nothing's ever gone wrong. We just sit and watch TV, then she goes to sleep, and I watch TV until her parents get home. But, I don't know, sometimes I get scared that something'll happen. I get scared that I'll screw it up: She'll get sick, and there won't be time for the ambulance to get there, and I won't know what to do, or I'll do something wrong, and she'll die or something. I watch that show "Rescue 911" and it's like, I can just picture that happening to me. I had a nightmare once. We were eating and she started to choke, and I put my hands around her like you're supposed to do but it didn't work. She started turning blue and everything, and she died. Her parents said it was my fault, and the police came for me. It was just a dream, but it *could* happen.

*Jessie, also 13, was a professional far beyond her years. For months I had hoped to meet just such a teen, one who had the experience to offer a ready opinion on the way kids have changed, and are changing:*

I baby-sit a lot. I get about $3.50, $4 an hour. I took the course and everything. It's usually pretty easy. But I was baby-sitting seven kids a few months ago; I was feeding the smallest one in the kitchen, in his high chair, and another one—he was in the middle of toilet training—was in the bathroom. He was taking forever in the bathroom, so I went to check on him. Of course he had dirtied his pants, and of course he was smearing it all over the floor. Just as I started to clean him up I heard a smash from the kitchen. The baby had slid out of his high chair and fallen on the floor. I called my mom, and she ran over. The baby was bleeding a little bit, but he was fine—didn't have to go to the hospital or anything. But it was scary.

*It's not* that *long ago you had baby-sitters yourself. Have you noticed that kids are different now, that eight- or nine-year-olds are different than you were at that age?*

They're a lot different. It seems like every year they get older. I mean, a seven-year-old this year behaves like an eight-year-old would have last year. Does that make sense? They're just *older*. They're also spoiled, most of the time. It also makes a difference if their parents aren't divorced. Some of the kids I sit for aren't divorced yet. They will be soon, but not yet.

Most of the kids either have parents that are divorced or a mother that works, or both. About 9 out of 10. So it ends up that they're not really close to their parents. The kids live in their bedrooms now; it wasn't like that when I was little. Their mom's at work and their father's gone, so they have these bedrooms with a television, a video machine, stereo, computer, and, of course, the biggest one of all, Nintendo. It makes baby-sitting a lot easier, though; the kids are happy enough just to sit in front of that stupid Nintendo thing all night long.

Kids now are completely independent—they do everything themselves—they don't need to be entertained like we did. They know how everything works. You don't have to cook for them because, if they're hungry, they just go into the kitchen and zap something in the microwave, or they just pick up the phone and call Domino's. A lot of parents leave money for pizza. There's never any kind of real dinner.

*Is it good that they're independent, or sad that they're, in a way, missing out on the traditional childhood?*

I guess it's sad, but that's just the way it is. That's what happens when the mother and father aren't there. On weekends, sometimes I think the kids I sit for really hate me. I think they think, "Hey, this is Saturday. I want my parents, not you."

*Some very insightful comments. Jessie brought out very accurately how the change in the traditional family has affected young children; how they have become more independent as the result of less time spent with their parents. There are those who approve of these effects, who respect small children already wise to the ways of the world. There is something to be said for it, but I want a child who runs up and down the hall with a Batman cape on, trying to fly. I don't want a child who picks up the telephone, dials his dentist, and makes an appointment to have his teeth cleaned. If that means I have to stay at home, I'd do it. Of course, I say this at a time in my life when I have no children, no wife; a time when all my worldly possessions are heaped in room 118 of the Howard Johnson's in Denver, Colorado.*

*I left Denver and began driving northeast. At about two in the morning, somewhere around Salt Lake City, a deer jumped out in front of my car and forced me to within one foot of a very steep cliff. Shaking, I pulled into a gas station-diner-motel and told the story to the very fat man I had just woken up. He said it happened all the time. Then he said there was only one room left and that it was a double. He charged me a ridiculous price to stay in a moldy cage for five hours.*

*It was then that I began losing my enthusiasm for life on the road. I thought how nice it would be to stay in one place long enough to memorize my telephone number. The charm of truck-stop cafés and local tourist attractions was fading. My car was ill, and I never wanted to see myself again. I had a sudden case of the truck-stop blues. I got on I-84 and plowed toward Portland, Oregon, stopping only for gas.*

# 13

# Portland, Oregon

*"Who are some famous people from Oregon?"*
*"There ain't none."*

*This 10-year-old's reply set the mood for my stay in Portland. I checked into the Best Western in the northwest part of town, where the Boys and Girls Club awaited me. The area was drab and out of focus. Paint was chipped; street signs were bent. The entire place seemed to me in a state of degradation. And this was not a* bad *part of town.*

*The neighborhood was lower middle class—small white houses shoulder to shoulder. At every major intersection there was a convenience store and a fast-food restaurant. Some of the kids at the club were brought there from the more dangerous areas, where drugs and gangs have made it unsafe to play outside. All over Portland the drug and gang situation was exploding. Again I heard all about the Crips and the Bloods.*

*The kids were runny-nosed and sluggish. They did nothing. They were "hangin'" and "kickin' it" and "chillin'." They passed the hours by throwing rocks at trees and terrorizing the younger kids.*

*I like kids. All through the trip I enjoyed meeting and talking to them, regardless of what they had to say. If they weren't pleasant, charming, or interesting they could still be provocative and compelling. They always had something to offer. Three days' worth of kids in Portland put this tenet to the test. They did have interesting things to say, but their sloppy style, their lack of concern, and their disrespect for me (one kid actually walked out in the middle of his interview when he saw a friend through the window) made it hard to get close to them—and I didn't make as great an effort as I had in other places. Some of these kids had it bad, but it was difficult to sympathize with them the way I had with previous kids. Most were back-porch kids, going nowhere—bent stop signs. I felt over this neighborhood and all its youthful inhabitants an overwhelming sense of inertia and stagnation.*

*Perhaps my own weariness contributed to this feeling. Had Portland been the first stop on my trip, I might have made an extra effort, might have seen the city in a brighter light. But I doubt it. As it was, I only left the Best Western for interviews. I mention all this because it affected the way in which I conducted these interviews. I guided the conversations into dark corners.*

*Wayne, six, was my first interview. He was a chubby kid, and his Batman T-shirt pulled tightly across his chest and fell short of his belt:*

I'm just six. I'm in first grade. You look just like my dad; you look just like him. But I got a new dad because my dad was touching my sister in the wrong way, and so my mom, she told my real dad that he had to leave. When we got outta the foster home we went back to my mom, and then I got my bike stolen and I got it back, and then it got stolen again and I didn't know who stole it.

My dad came to my school. He came to my school, and they had to call the police. He found out where we lived and he came to my house, and he came and tried to take us away from my mom, and my mom says he wants to hurt us or kill us. *(He takes his shirt off.)* I gotta take my shirt off because I'm hot. And when I was at the foster home my tooth fell out and I got money from the tooth fairy.

But my mom got a new daddy for us and he's nice; and I know his name. His name is Warren, but I call him Daddy Warren. If he meets my dad they'll get in a fight. I think Daddy Warren'll kill my dad if they ever see each other. When my face gets red, that means I'm overheated and I have to take my shirt off.

*His brother, Dennis, a seven-year-old, confirmed the story and then added:*

Things are better without my dad around, but my mom gets real mad sometimes. She got mad when I jumped off the roof and hurt my leg. I hate it when she tells me what to do. If I had a lot of power I'd go into a spaceship and tell the Martians they had to clean everything up and cook for me.

*Jamie was nine. He had a cowlick and pink-rimmed eyes, and I remember thinking that he would be any bully's favorite target:*

I'm a quiet person. I just like to read; I like it better than being with other kids. I like fairy tales. I like them because nothing bad ever happens; it's always happy in the end.

The boys here beat me up all the time. They're mean. They think they're real hotshots. They think that Martin Luther King said all of it, so they think they can take over the world now. . . . Yes, it's the black boys that beat me up. No white kids do that. Plus, they only pick on kids that are littler than them. I've got a twin brother, and they pick on him too. They know that we're not strong enough to beat 'em. I wish I was. Sometimes I wish I could just beat 'em all up so they'd never bother me again.

There's one of 'em that's the worst: Carl. He already beat me up today—he beats me up every day. He punched me in the stomach this morning, for no reason. He's fourteen, and I'm only nine. He thinks he's the boss.

White people are nice, but the black kids think they can take over the world. I have one black friend, and that's it. They want to be the strongest, you know? They want to show that they're stronger than whites. They want to show that they can tell whites what to do. That's why they pick on me. They can beat me up and make fun of me, and they know I'm not strong enough to do anything about it.

Sometimes I think it would be nice to show 'em, you know? I'd like to see them all get beat up and cry by someone older than them. A white guy. That'd show 'em.

*I talked to Gabby, a real young 12-year-old, outside in the parking lot. On the other side of the lot there was an Arctic Circle, a local fast-food joint. I could barely hear her over the drive-through loudspeaker:*

Kids make fun of me. All the kids here make fun of me. They say I stink; they call me a nerd; they make fun of the things I do; they make fun of my shoes, my clothes. Even, like today I'm wearing a "New Kids" T-shirt, and they say, "Oh, New Fags on the Block!" They never stop teasing me. They make me cry sometimes. But what am I gonna do? I can't fight them, and I'm not gonna make fun of them back. I don't like hurting people's feelings. I try to do everything I can—I have my mom's Camp Beverly Hills perfume on today. Smell.

School's bad too. I don't have any—I have one friend that's so special, but I haven't seen her in a long time. *(The loudspeaker screams: "Double Arctic burger, fries, Dr. Pepper!")* I miss her *so* much. I dedicated a song to her on the radio, but I don't think she heard it. She was such a good friend.

That was back in Utah, where we lived before this. We moved here last year, and I haven't seen her or talked to her since. I remember when I first met her. I was walking to school and I fell in a puddle, and I was just sitting there; I didn't know what to do 'cause I was all wet. Then Carolyn—that's her name—and her father came by, and they picked me up, and he drove us both to school. After that we were best friends. We did everything together. I'd go over to her house to play, and we'd play Tarzan off her porch for hours. We had so much *fun*!

I had a crossing guard in Utah that I liked a lot. *Every day* when I came to cross by the school she'd say, "Close your eyes and hold out your hand," and I'd do it, and she'd put a piece of candy in it, or something. *("Arctic fillet o' fish burger, strawberry shake, onion rings!")* One day, on the way home, she gave me a cherry Slurpee. She was *so* sweet! It was just me, no one else.

*(A little girl comes over to see what is going on, and Gabby turns on her brutally: "Excuse me! Excuse me! Can't you see that we're busy? Get out!")*

But anyway, I've lived in three places before Portland, so I'm a little used to leaving my friends. When you go into a new school, you're always the one kids make fun of. I guess that's why they say I stink here. I wish I could go back to Utah. It's not really fair when you think about it. I was happy there, and I had friends and everything; but I really don't like it here, and no one likes me. So why am I here?

*Tony, nine, was my favorite—he reminded me of Teddy, the Don Juan of the Minneapolis Boys and Girls Club. He was on vacation from Milwaukee.*

I think I'm weird. I don't really know what other people think . . . I just think I'm *weird.* Well, I like bugs and stuff. I really like ants and grasshoppers.

I like doing testing, testing things, and doing experiments. I found out how long it takes to kill a potato bug—that's one of those ugly little things that can turn itself into a little gray ball—it takes two minutes. About two minutes.

*How did you do it?*

I stuck a piece of rusty metal in its stomach.

*What other things are weird about you?*

Well, sometimes I talk to the bugs I keep at home. My mom says that's weird.

*What do the girls think about your being weird?*

Well . . . there's one girl now, Dierdra, that really likes me, but she's a little weird herself. She's got freckles and she likes to go messin' around with boys. She'll go kickin' 'em in the butt and stuff like that when they're playin' soccer. I like her, but I'm only here for the summer, visiting my dad. I live in Milwaukee.

The other one's normal—my girlfriend back home. I think normal girls like weird boys. It's like, they think it's exciting. That's good for me.

*One of the counselors convinced Ricardo, 14, to talk to me. Once we started, he said that it felt like being in court. He was a political zealot:*

I like rap music because, I think 90 percent of the rappers are rapping about *not* doing drugs and not joining gangs. I think they're real important. It's black people that suffer the most from drugs and gangs; and it's only black people that're gonna help black people. I don't live in a bad neighborhood, and I got a good education—private school and everything—that gives me, like, a different perspective. I think the government fuels all the problems black people have. I think they supply the gangbangers with guns and money and everything, so they can throw off the blacks, kill off all the blacks. A lot of people think that. That's why a lot of rappers are turning against it, and turning to Africalistic things: African clothes, black medallions, African subjects.

I can understand the government, in a way. This isn't my nation; I don't belong here. I belong back in Africa. If I had some money I'd go now. You got to recognize your roots. The African-American movement is getting much bigger; the NAACP is getting much more involved; people are reading Malcolm X.

White people are just fooling themselves if they think African-Americans are treated equally. It's still like, a white person's normal and a black person's black. That's why we gotta keep on moving ahead. We gotta build more black colleges and help the people in the ghettos. But they gotta help themselves, too. It makes me sick to see the African-Americans sitting around the ghettos on welfare, doing nothing to try and get a better life.

*It doesn't help the kids when role models, like basketball and football players, keep going to jail for drugs. Why do you think so many of these guys that make it out just can't stay out of trouble?*

They come from the ghetto. They make a lot of money, and they don't know what to do with it. They go crazy. It's rough in the ghetto. You can't just make a lot of money and then say, "Yeah, I'm OK now."

*Tammy, 11, was a commuter. She spoke, slowly and deliberately, of the effect gang violence and drugs have had on her neighborhood:*

I live in the northeast part of Portland. It's a pretty bad neighborhood . . . Bloods, Crips . . . we're gonna move. There's a lot of guns, shootings . . . it's scary to walk around the block. You gotta make sure you're not wearin' the wrong color.

I think kids are growin' up too fast. I seen little kids in my neighborhood all the time, they're playin' with blood needles and condoms that they find on the street; little kids pickin' up condoms and puttin' them in their mouth, and they been used before. That's when you know somethin's wrong. I found one—a blood needle—when I was little, and I didn't really know what it was, and I stuck myself with it, and I had to go get all these shots and everything. I'm lucky I didn't get AIDS.

No one has respect for nothin'; no respect for other people and no respect for themselves. They just do whatever they want because the police never come in our neighborhood anyway—only if someone got shot or somethin'. It's the parents, too. They don't give their kids no help. They don't even care where they are or what they're doin'. They don't tell their kids not to play with blood needles, and if they get stuck the parents don't even do anything.

From the tone of Tammy's voice it's obvious she feels cheated. She is all but pleading, "I don't want to live in that neighborhood. Why can't I live in a better place?"

I think the neighborhood means a lot. I mean, *now*. if you're a little black kid growin' up in my neighborhood, you don't have a chance, you know. You got blood needles for toys; you got shootings and crime all over; and you grow up wantin' to be a gangbanger. I'm OK, but kids growin' up now . . . you walk down the street and drunk people be talkin' to you. Kids shouldn't have to deal with that. All the gang people come out in the street at night and drink and party and stuff. I'm not allowed out of the house after seven. The whole place looks bad; the houses are all fallin' apart, and people can't afford to fix 'em. Even the drug dealers—they got money—they just let their houses stay all messed up. But they got a real expensive car parked out front.

I like talkin' to white people best, hangin' around with white people, because where they live, there's not so much goin' on. You don't gotta worry 'bout needles. That's why I come here to the club. It's real safe here.

*Keisha, 13, told me she wasn't into gangs anymore. But she was wearing an L. A. Raiders football jacket in the heat of July:*

*What's with that jacket?*

*(Laughs.)* I ain't no gangbanger. I just like the jacket. I couldn't even wear it in school. They don't allow it.

The Crips and the Bloods got here about two years ago or somethin'. I know a lot of 'em that came here from California, but there's some from here who went down to L. A. and just brought it back with 'em: "*Maaaan*, I just come back from California and there's Crips and stuff. . . ." It just happened. The neighborhood I live in used to be all Crips that hanged around, until Arthur got shot. He was the leader. Some Bloods just drove by and killed 'im. Now all the Crips are in different sets and stuff. The police are there too.

Bein' in gangs is real popular around here. Everybody wants to be in. Kids run aroun' playin' gang stuff. They get in as soon as they old enough. I used to be all into it. I used to run around claimin' Crip, 'cause all my cousins did, and they used to go with some Crips. I was around 'em all the time. I got initiated by some little Crips, luckily, wannabe gangsters. *(The standard initiation consists of fighting your way through the set you're claiming).* I know a guy got initiated so bad he had to go in the hospital for a week. But now I don't claim nothin' anymore. Too much killin's. I just left. I know you can't do that in California; everyone in your set'll beatcha up. It ain't like that here, and I was just a little Crip anyway. That was last year.

Downtown's real bad. There's a lotta shootin'—the real stuff, not like the wannabes out here. But since Ray got shot the whole thing's just gettin' bigger.

I ain't religious, not yet anyhow. I don't wanna go to church or stay in at night. I'm a kid; I wanna have fun. I wanna stay out real late and go to parties and go to the movies and stuff. The gang parties are the best; there's a lotta people and stuff . . . Look! *(She points out the window to a boy wearing a jacket like hers.)* That's Damon. He's in my class. That fool's crippin' real hard.

*Cheyanne, 16, looked as if she was on the lam. Her entire body was hidden; her head by a gray bandana, her face by dark glasses, her neck to her knees by an enormous, flowing windbreaker, and her feet and calves by olive army boots.*

*She described how easily—or naturally—drugs and gangs are accepted:*

This whole place has changed since the Crips and the Bloods came here a couple a years ago. It's gotten bigger; it's changed everybody. Some of it's bad and some of it's good; the place is a lot more exciting now. You just gotta know how to handle it. There's a lotta girls that can't. They're just slaves to the gangsters. My high school's gettin' a day-care thing 'cause there's so many girls with babies, and it's all the gangbangers that got 'em pregnant. There's one guy I know who got, like, three girls pregnant in a year—and one of 'em was just 13. They're just fools. As soon as the gangbangers came all the girls were like, "Oh, I'm gonna get me one a them and get all rich" and everything. But they don't get nothin' outta it—they get pregnant and go on welfare and end givin' *him* the money. They're just stupid wannabes. I take precautions when I have sex. I ain't gonna have no baby when I'm 16. All these girls, they don't have abortions, and they get a baby, and the guy leaves, and they just leave it with their mother and forget all about it. I mean, they have competitions to see who can get the real high-rollers, the gangbangers that came up from Los Angeles—they'll do anything to get one a them. It's like goin' out with a movie star. But these guys are serious; cars, gold, everything. They don't have no girlfriend for too long.

I mean the gang guys are nice—the real ones, not the wannabes. You just gotta know how to handle it.

*But these guys get their money from selling drugs.*

There's nothin' wrong with a drug dealer. I mean, it's just the way it is. Drug dealers don't bother me. They're just ordinary people who sell drugs. . . . Yeah, the killin' is bad, that that's just a part of it too. I knew a boy got killed by another guy because he shot his dog—and they were both Crips. I knew both of 'em. He got shot three times. That's stupid. I claimed a set, I'm a Crip, I don't go around shootin' people. But I do carry a knife sometimes, 'cause, you never know what someone else might have. I've been in a few fights with other girls, but I never got hurt. But that's how people get killed: Someone pulls out a knife and then the other person pulls out a gun . . . or sometimes a couple a girls'll get in a fight and their boyfriends will find out about it and go lookin' for the other girl's boyfriend, and someone'll get killed. It's dangerous out there; I just heard about some Crips that got a whole bunch a guns from some army store in exchange for drugs—it can be dangerous.

My boyfriend's into it more than I am. He goes crosstown and hangs out with his cousins that are real gangsters. I tell him to be careful, but, that's just the way it is.

*There was a lot of talk about God. Most of the kids described themselves as religious, but they all seemed to cast God in a curious role. Nine-year-old Dennis said, "I like God. When I think about stealing something, He stops me."*

*It took a while for Vernon, a very reserved 15-year-old, to warm up. I think he was suspicious of me and my motives for conducting these interviews. After a half hour he was running the show by himself:*

Everyone keeps pretty much to their own group. I hang out with the other people that go to church and learn about Jesus. There's a lot of us, but there are lots of other groups: There are the blacks—the wannabes or the kids that are already gang members; the big sneakers, Air Jordans and stuff. They dress real sharp. Then you have the white kids who try to be gangsters; they shave their heads and wear Raiders jackets and do everything to try to be black. Then you have the Rockers, or the Stoners, the heavy-metal thing; they do a lot of drugs—smoke pot on the school bus—and they got real long hair and dirty jeans and they always have cigarettes in their hands. Part of that group is the girls—the real slutty ones—with black leather and stuff. The other slutty group is part of the upper-class group; they wear lots of makeup, and they do anything to be popular; and the rest of the upper-class is the preppy guys and the preppy girls. Then you have the jocks and the cheerleaders. All the rest are either the real smart ones who never say anything and the normal kids that dress normally and are nice and everything—I guess I'm in there.

Of all of them I guess the gangsters are the most popular. Everybody wants to be a gangster. My mother works with this lady whose son is a gangster, and she asked, "How can you let your son go around selling drugs?" and she said, "Do you think I can afford my house by myself? Do you think *I* bought that car out there?" She doesn't care; she's making money through him—real money. That's why the gangs are so popular, because you can get rich while you're in high school.

I just hang around with my friends and skateboard. And I go to church stuff a lot. My family's very religious; that's what keeps me safe. Me and my friends go to "skate church"; it's a church that has all these skateboard ramps in the basement. You can skate for an hour and a half, and then you get a half-hour—they teach you about the Bible for 30 minutes. It's good because it's learning about God and the Bible; it's not like preaching or anything. And when that's over you skate for a while. My father brings me there, and my friends and their parents come a lot, so it's great. It's bringing everybody closer to Jesus, and that's what really counts. My dad's responsible for a lot of it; he brought a lot of people in there. Everyone loves him. He's been off of drugs and alcohol for 10 months now, and he's lost about 40 pounds. He's doing great! He's involved in all of it; sometimes he leads discussions where people talk about what Jesus means to them or something. He's a great example for everyone because he's born-again, and look what it's done for him. It's a long way from shooting cocaine like he used to.

I really like skate church and the people that go there. And it's much nicer than getting beat up by gang members. My friend got pulled off his bike and kicked in the face; I got mugged last year by some Bloods; they pushed me around and stole my money. That stuff isn't for me.

*It seems perverse that these kids have to choose between the Crips and God. In the end they can't walk down the street without becoming a gang member, can't go skateboarding without Jesus.*

*I ate lunch in the Arctic Circle after my last interview, before hitting the road. There was a woman in the booth next to me eating alone. A bearded man came in, bought a coffee and scoped the place out. He spotted the woman and clumsily made his way over and introduced himself. He told her it was always nicer to drink coffee with company, and she agreed. Five minutes later these complete strangers were sharing their private lives.*

*The woman said that she was divorced and the man said so was he; his wife had run off with a guy she met at night school. The woman replied that she would be overjoyed if her ex-husband would run off, but he was still in the same neighborhood, living with a fat woman who sells perfume. He wouldn't even take the kids on the weekends.*

*The man sipped his coffee and sighed. The divorce has been tough on his kids, he said, and they couldn't understand why their mother left them. He was worried because he didn't know enough about children to take care of them by himself.*

*The woman said her kids were better off without their father. She scowled and called her ex-husband an animal. She said that his temper used to frighten the kids into running away.*

*The man concluded by saying that he believed in destiny. He thought there must be a reason why they had met and had this conversation. He knew his wife left him for a reason and he hoped that the woman could help him figure it all out. He left with her phone number.*

*Of course, a child is largely a reflection of his parents and his upbringing. It was easy to draw lines between these adults and the kids I had interviewed. When you have a parent seeking psychoanalysis in the Arctic Circle, you can bet that somewhere close there's a very confused child.*

# 14

# Los Angeles, California

*About 30 miles north of the Oregon-California border I passed my 48th and final official weigh-in station for trucks. Of the 48, 2 were open.*

*It was the middle of July and I was driving the home stretch. I decided to enjoy that last leg of my trip. I drove slowly, I stopped often, and took in local sights. I drove the Redwood Highway over the border to Highway 101, which wiggles all the way down the coast to Los Angeles. I walked around the Redwood National Park. I followed signs to the world's largest tree house. I stopped in Eureka, where nearly 200 years ago Americans struck it rich and built the West.*

*In L.A. I met kids through all manner of personal and professional contacts. Having lived in Los Angeles I had no trouble arranging interviews. I talked to several kids in Venice, home of the famous boardwalk (without boards) and home of some of the most overtly deranged souls in the universe. Venice also contains some dangerous drug-and gang-ridden areas. As in other cities, even the very young kids were touched by the violence.*

*These first few kids were in the middle of it: economically depressed; stuck in project housing, where crime is never far away. Amy, seven, rambled in the same singsong way most seven-year-olds do, but the subject was far from Disneyland:*

My daddy saved me from the gangbangers when I was little. They came by shooting and some bullets hit the wall. On *my* street there's a *whole bunch* a gangbangers. They shoot at people and sell *drugs*. They shoot at people for *no* reason. They shot a girl from my school in her *arm* when she was playin' on the *sidewalk*, and they *killed* a boy on my street 'cause he was a Blood.

I was ridin' my bike with my friend, and we drove by these kids, and I *thought* one of 'em was my friend, but he *wasn't*. He was my friend's brother, and he hangs out with the Crips. They threw *mud* at us, and they pushed my friend right off her bike. They're *mean*, 'cause they want to be Crips when they grow up.

I like my mom though. She says I can walk home from school if I want.

*What does your mom do?*

She used to do *drugs*, but she doesn't anymore, since my daddy moved back with us. She went to these meetings and she got *sober*. When she was doin' drugs I went to live with my *aunt*. My daddy called, and he said he was comin' to *visit* me, but he *didn't come*. I went out on the back porch with my clothes. "If he doesn't come in five minutes, I'm gonna run away forever." He never came, but I fell asleep 'cause I was *real* tired 'cause it was 10 o'clock. When I woke up I was just *surrounded* by *gangbangers*! I wanna go to India, 'cause they don't have gangbangers there. I'd be more safer there.

*Wilton was only nine and a half:*

Shit yeah, I wanna be a gangbanger. That's it, you know. I got to admit it: I love fightin'; I love the Crips; I wanna kill Bloods. I know I might get killed—that's a part of it—that's why you gotta have heart, 'cause when you claim a set, it's like family. And if I gotta die, that's the way I wanna go: bullets flyin' all over the place, smoke, screamin' . . . yeah, that's it, man.

*Leroy, seven, told me he wanted to be a cop, and I thought, "Oh, that's a nice thing to hear in this kind of atmosphere." Then he told me* why *he wanted to be a cop:*

You get to arrest people, and sometimes, if they run away, you can shoot 'em. I'm gonna be one of those cops, who drives around, in a car with no lights on it, so no one knows, I'm a cop.

I'm gonna shoot bad guys—I saw a guy, on my street, and he had a gun. I told my mom, and she called the police, and they said, "Thanks for saying that." Those are the guys I'll shoot. I'll arrest the people, the ones in the street, the ones who talk when I'm sleeping. And all the gangbangers, and the ones who sell crack, all the ones wearing L.A. Raider hats, and jackets. I'll put 'em all in jail, one by one, and they'll never know that I'm a cop.

*I met Rick when he was playing with a bunch of 10-year-olds after school. Because he himself was 16 I found it odd. He had a frayed shirt and filthy white Levis; his hair was still flat on one side from his pillow:*

Venice High is a zoo. The work is easy, but there are lots of fights and gangs and drugs. You can buy any kind of drug you want at my school.

I live with my dad and my grandmother. My grandmother cleans up the house and stuff, and my dad's on welfare. . . . No, I don't feel too good about welfare. I want my dad to work. We don't have enough money for clothes and stuff—just food; and since he's been on welfare he just sits around watching TV. I don't think he likes welfare too much either. He's been out of work for five, six years.

I had a job last summer at the hospital, taking out the trash and doing the linen and stuff. I bought school clothes and food. It's better to *buy* food instead of using food stamps.

I just wanna get of out school and get a real job so I don't end up like my father.

*Xavier, 13, introduced himself to me and claimed to be the most interesting kid in the neighborhood. He told me that talking to any other kid would be a waste of time:*

Yeah, I call the 900 numbers a lot. It's fun, you know. It's, like, the only way to talk to real girls, and not the girls my age. They're real dirty, real experienced. I call the party lines too, 'cause there you can talk to other people like you, not just the ones who get paid for doin' it. I wanna meet a girl on the party line and meet her somewhere and get down to it, you know what I mean?

*Warren, 15, was so stoned when I talked to him that out of a half-hour interview only the following two paragraphs were intelligible:*

I smoke a lot of weed—well, not a lot, once or twice a day—'cause I like what it does for me, you know. It's good to smoke a little before school 'cause, like, that's the only way you can make it through the day. That's when I smoke—before school—and then after school, to cool down from it all.

That's why I don't like hearin' all this stuff about weed's gonna kill ya, you know, 'cause it's weed that keeps *me* goin' all day long. If I couldn't smoke, I'd never be able to make it through school. Man, not only should they make it legal, they should sell it in the school cafeteria too.

*Also in Venice I met Rannie, 16, who lived with his father in a very expensive house overlooking the boardwalk. His room was a mess, and my tape recorder actually stuck to his desk:*

My parents put me into a private school a few years ago. I wanted to go to Venice High, but to survive in that place you gotta be either a surfer, a football player, or a gang member. My school's pretty calm. Kids are pretty normal, including me.

One thing I haven't told too many people, is, I tried crack once. Eighth grade, when I was 13. I was with my best friend, in his house, and he had this older brother that was, like, the kinda guy who was always in trouble. He was about 17, and he had just started getting into crack. Me and my friend smoked a little pot back then, but we were well-educated people, and we knew that crack was a big deal. But at the same time we were curious. We wanted to try it.

It was a great high. I loved it. Everything was speeded up. We were all peppy, talking real fast. It came over me really quickly—and it wasn't harsh to smoke or anything—and it ended real quickly. That's why it's such a big problem: When you come out of it, you want to get high again, immediately. It was scary in that sense, because I could understand how people get hooked and just ruin their lives—it's amazingly addictive. We smoked everything he had, and I wanted more. But I was expecting that. I didn't smoke anymore; I haven't smoked since, and I'll never do it again. But I'm kind of glad I did it that once.

*Maria, 12, was very happy living where she did; in the Hollywood hills. My work in L.A. would have been incomplete had I not found at least one aspiring actress-dancer-singer:*

This is a good place for me to live because I wanna be in show business. I've already started; I sing at Shakey's Pizza sometimes. They have a little corner of the restaurant where people can sing on weekends, and a deejay. The deejay chooses who can sing again, and she chose me and said I should get an agent and start singing professionally. When I was in there I sang "That's What Friends Are For" and "Like a Virgin." For a while I wanted to be a veterinarian, but I think singing would be more fun than going to medical school. You don't have to *know* anything to be a singer. You just sing. And you get lots of attention, which is nice.

My stepdad took me to see Whitney Houston, and she was just *fabulous*.

*Independence has its price; about one third of all teens now work to support their life-styles. I talked with Devin, a 16-year-old burger flipper, at his mother's apartment in South Hollywood:*

I got this job at Kentucky Fried Chicken—in the back, you know; I ain't no cashier or nothin'. I don't mind workin' there so long ain't no one sees my face. I mean, ain't no one gonna see me wearin' this stupid uniform. No way. I stay in the back and make the food and stock shit up.

The thing is, I don't wanna work, but I got to; I need the money. My family ain't poor or nothin', but they don't have enough money to give me, you know. If I want somethin' I gotta get it myself. And you gotta have stuff, you know, like the right clothes—a new pair of Air Jordans costs more'n a hundred bucks. You gotta buy food when you're out. You gotta be able to buy things for girls if you're out, like food or tickets for the movie or whatever. If you can't handle all that shit they you ain't goin' nowhere, you know what I mean? Like, you ain't nothin' if you wearin' the same clothes and shoes and you ain't got no cash to spend. It ain't fun bein' nothin'. Course, I don't know nothin' 'bout that. *(Laughs.)*

*Dorthe was the 16-year-old product of an American artist and a Danish writer. She had spent most of her 16 years in Copenhagen but spoke perfect English. She was to stay in Santa Monica for the rest of her secondary schooling. Like every other European teen, Dorthe was an environmentalist:*

The Santa Monica Bay is to the point now where you need a knife and fork if you want to swim. They even say it's not safe. There's a big sewer pipe that drains garbage straight out into the bay, right where the people are swimming!

The thing is, the thing that's so typical of Americans is, that everybody complains about it—they scream because they can't go surfing—but nobody's willing to start cleaning up after themselves. It's like they don't understand that it's their own fault. They don't understand that when you take your McDonald's styrofoam containers and throw them out on the side of the road, that they're gonna end up in the ocean, or in a waste dump. No one includes themself in the problem.

It's like night and day going from Copenhagen to Los Angeles. In Copenhagen we recycle everything: bottles, newspapers, glass; we have trucks that come around to collect your old batteries. We've been recycling forever. It just makes me so mad! In Denmark we do so much to help the environment. It's so natural we don't even think about it. Americans would never even think about doing it. Not the average American anyway. They assume someone else will come along and do it for them. I'm half-American, but in conversations like this I just say I'm Danish.

*I knew I was coming to the end of my interviews. I asked Lilly, a 12-year-old from Mar Vista, what she thought of her life:*

It's weird; my mom had a hard life, you know, the way it used to be for most people. She was born in Germany and had to escape to Israel because of the Nazis. Then she had to live on a kibbutz, 'cause her father died when she was 14. And here I am in L.A. I have nice clothes, and I go to a private school.

*Do you think the world is better now than it was when your mom was your age?*

I think it wasn't good then and it isn't good now, but sometime in between it was pretty good. *(Laughs.)* She had the Nazis; we have gangs, drugs, and pollution. But things were real calm in the middle: '50s music, the Fonz—like it was in *Back to the Future.*

I went to the Griffith Park observatory with my mom, and she said she could remember when you could see the whole town, instead of just a glob of haze and smog.

*Finally I talked to Ruth, a 16-year-old from the beach of Santa Monica. On my way to her apartment I passed a surfer van, a Volkswagen bus so decrepit I dared not get too close. Looking back as I passed I saw a message spray-painted on the back door: "Don't laugh, your daughter might be in here." What a terrifying thought. I don't have a daughter, but I don't want anyone talking about her like that.*

*I expected Ruth to be guilty by association—she shared the same beach with the surfers—but she was nothing of the kind. In fact, she reminded me of Myrna Loy in* The Bachelor and the Bobbysoxer: *strong, intelligent, almost stoic, yet vulnerable and sensitive:*

People think I'm weird because I like to read a lot. Nobody reads anymore—I can't believe what's happening to this country, how conservative it's getting. Censorship, abortion, flag burning;

they're pulling books off of school-library shelves. People were ready to kill Rosanne Barr because she made a joke that involved the national anthem. It was a joke, for Christ's sake! I didn't like it either, 'cause I think she's disgusting, but a joke is a joke. It's so scary to think that religious freaks and ignorant southerners have so much power. They boycott movies and records without even seeing or hearing them. It's the stupid Republicans; they turned the country backwards.

I was just reading that some schools aren't letting kids in if they're wearing Bart Simpson T-shirts, because they say he symbolizes laziness and underachievement. He's a cartoon character!

The satanic lyrics thing. Some kid in some back-ass farming place kills himself after listening to heavy metal. How healthy do you think this kid was *before* he turned on the record player? If his mother hadn't been preaching to him and his father hadn't been molesting him in the barn, or something like that, I don't think the lyrics would have bothered him so much.

The whole thing is so frustrating. I'm 16 years old—I hate when I see some mayor from Mississippi being interviewed on CNN and I think, "Christ! *I* make more sense than that!"

*I really liked Ruth. This girl could change the world. She reminded me a little of myself and my friends in our early days of cynicism. Ruth seemed to have a bead on it all. I suppose that if kids are subject to adult circumstances, there must be some 16-year-olds out there capable of seeing through adults and adult things. In this way, Ruth was a nice interview to finish with. It was also a fitting interview with which to lead into some afterthoughts on my drive across America.*

# Afterthoughts

Kids *do* grow up fast these days. Their horizons are broader; they are exposed to more, do more, and seem in greater jeopardy than previous generations.

Kids have changed because the environment has changed. In school they are surrounded by computers. They are taught about AIDS and the perils of drug abuse, and guidance counselors help them overcome the grief of losing classmates to suicide. There are even baby-sitters for students with children.

Today's kids are threatened by more and greater dangers. Drugs are traded like baseball cards, and kids who yield to peer pressure now smoke crack, not cigarettes. Violence is in. Child molesters cruise the suburbs and pedophiles open day-care centers. The Crips and the Bloods have turned schools, streets, and parks into the Old West. In many areas, kids have to stay inside for safety. No one walks to school anymore, at least not alone.

In the last 20 years, constant parental supervision has given way to relative autonomy. And the concept of the family has changed. Mothers have joined the work force, and despite the additional income, parents work long hours to feed their families or pay soaring tuition fees in times of increasing economic uncertainty. There are latchkey kids and after-school-program kids who only see their parents on the weekends. There are microwave enchiladas and delicious shakes where the turkey and mashed potatoes used to be.

With these adultlike circumstances and pressures in their day-to-day lives, and without their parents around to help, kids are forced to accept an early independence. They feel they have to solve their own problems. They make adult decisions, live adult lives. They flip burgers to support hobbies and habits, and go about the business of survival and promotion. They relieve stress in the same ways adults do: music, sports, sex, 900 numbers, drugs, God, exercise.

The result of all this is a more extreme generation. A youth with fierce direction, resolve, and resilience, just as capable of setting new standards of achievement as they are of systematically destroying themselves.

I'm not a critic of the new generation and its influences, nor am I a critic of contemporary parenting. I don't believe the family has broken down so much as it has changed. Times change. In a way the potential is very exciting. The Simpsons and the Bundys have replaced the Waltons. A new era has begun.

But I do worry about the kids. The times have changed very quickly, and many of these kids just aren't ready to be adults.

My trip across America was a long journey and a personal success. I achieved what I set out to: to discover the new breed of children. In fact, my only disappointment was the lack of regional diversity. I expected kids in different places to behave differently, but they didn't, to any significant degree. There was a sameness about their values and attitudes that can only be attributed to the shrinking of America. A friend of mine calls it the McDonald's syndrome, because regardless of who you are and where you are, you're never more than five minutes away from a Big Mac. Nowadays, kids eat the same fast food, sing the same songs, and watch the same shows. The Teenage Mutant Ninja Turtles and Madonna are heroes common to all regions.

The other striking similarity I found is that everywhere, at every social strata, kids seem automatically to assume that their problems are their own. They are remarkably self-reliant, with little or no sense of being able to turn to adults for help.

The kids I met provided me with many experiences worthy of reflection, and I had ample time to reflect upon them. I developed personal views on child rearing, and I recognize an increasing anxiousness to apply them to my own children. As I was finishing this book, I reached a firm decision:

I want my kids to be independent, self-reliant, and strong, but always to know that they have the family for a support system.

My children will be born in Charleston, where they will spend carefree hours walking into trees and playing in the sand. They will undergo primary and secondary schooling in Minneapolis, where they will play ice hockey and skate in the winter and spend the summers near the lake reading the classics. Eventually, they will attend Columbia University—or perhaps just live in New York City, and become adults. After that it's up to them.

# Encores

Not all the kids I talked to found a home in the preceding chapters. Some passages, despite their pointedness and humor, simply could not be worked into the narrative. Still, I couldn't bear to let them go, so I saved my favorite bits and pieces, and they are grouped by subject over the following pages.

For me, these are snapshots, souvenirs of my trip; a scrapbook that puts into perspective my five months and my 300 kids.

## The Future

**Julie**
**8 years old**
**Los Angeles, CA**

I wanna be a singer when I grow up—or a ballet teacher. I don't wanna sit at a desk all day doin' paperwork, you know, 'cause I'm one of those wild kids. That's why I don't like school. It's *soooo* boring. It's all work, and I don't like working. I wanna have fun—I *don't* wanna sit at a desk all day.

**Edward**
**10 years old**
**St. Paul, MN**

I think the worst thing about being an adult is dying. I don't want to get older. I don't want to grow up, because then you have to die.

**George**
**14 years old**
**Memphis, TN**

I wanna be rich. I'm smart, you know, so I know I'll make a lot a money. I'll go to college, and then I figure it'll take three years. Real estate. Lamborghini, Ferrari, big house, boat, pool. After a few years of that I'll get married and start a family.

# Fear

**Sally**
**7 years old**
**Denver, CO**

When I was smaller I used to get afraid that I wouldn't find my way home from school. That I'd be walking around forever. I have bad dreams sometimes; dreams like, I didn't know there were people coming to get me. I scream for help, but there's nobody there.

**Jeffrey**
**10 years old**
**East Brunswick, NJ**

Sometimes I don't like playing Little League—like when a pop fly comes, then I don't like it. If there's two outs and it's important and everything, I just, like, pray that the ball won't come to me. I did it once, dropped a fly ball . . . everyone yelled at me and made fun of me and stuff. They yell at me like I didn't try or nothin'.

**Dwayne**
**13 years old**
**Portland, OR**

There's this girl, Ginger, in my class. She's real . . . she's real . . . you know. I know she likes me—I know it, and I've liked her for a long time. But she doesn't, like, come over and talk to me.

*Why don't you talk to her?*

Are you kidding?

# Brothers and Sisters and Friends

**Tammara**
**7 years old**
**Princeton, NJ**

Sometimes my sister goes to birthday parties and I don't get to go. She has a lot more friends than I do. . . . Well, I think it's because there are lots of kids in her school. I have friends there too, but I don't go there anymore.

*What about the kids in your new school?*

Well, they don't invite me. They invite other people. I have two friends from my old school, but I don't get to see them anymore. Every once in a while the kids in my new school make fun of me. They don't like me like my old friends did.

**Albert**
**9 years old**
**St. Louis Park, MN**

I don't like girls. One minute they say this, and the next minute they say something else. They always try to get things from you, you know, like, "Well, if you trade your apple for this I'll. . . ." I think I'll probably get married someday. But the girl I marry'll have to be different from the ones at school.

**Patrice**
**10 years old**
**Charleston, SC**

I'm the one in the whole class that gets more boyfriends than anyone else. These two boys came to the door a few days ago when we were eatin' breakfast and they asked if we wanted to walk to school with them and we said no.

*Does that make them boyfriends?*

Well, yeah, kinda. There's a couple of boys—they sent someone to tell me they liked me and wanted to be my boyfriend, so they're my boyfriends too. . . . No, I don't talk to them; they're in different classes. I have one real boyfriend that I talk to in school. My mom won't let us go out or nothin'. He gave me his I.D. bracelet. That means it's, like, serious. You've got to wear it all the time.

*But you're not wearing a bracelet.*

Well, it's kinda ugly. I wear it to school or if I know he's gonna be around. He's a real funny guy; he looks like one of the Simpsons. He's got this one friend, Nicholas, but he says, like, "Hey Niggerless, what's up?" *(Laughs.)*

**Danny**
**13 years old**
**La Crosse, WI**

I like to write poetry. I write poems for my best friend to give to his girlfriend. She eats it up. I don't have a girlfriend, so it's not like I'm wasting 'em or nothing. He pays me back by taking out the garbage and things like that. Lets me borrow his roller blades.

# Family

**Jed**
**10 years old**
**Myrtle Beach, SC**

I don't like my big brother. He thinks he's real big and real bad. He's always tryin' to tell me what to do and toss me around. I hit him with a book yesterday.

*Have you ever tried smashing him on the head with a toaster?*

Hmmmm . . . no, but I throwed a hammer at him once.

**Leona**
**8 years old**
**Hartford, CT**

My mom works in a department store, on the fifth floor. I don't know anything about my dad, 'cause when I was born he ran off. My mom's boyfriend is much better. I don't really want to meet my dad. I mean, why should I? He doesn't deserve to get us back.

**Kelly**
**7 years old**
**Bloomington, MN**

I like being an only child. I don't have to worry about my older brother or sister picking on me. I wouldn't mind having a younger sister though, so I could pick on her. If I broke a vase in the house I could just say that she did it.

**Gina**
**7 years old**
**Somerville, NJ**

My dad does something but I forget what it's called . . . physics . . . he does physics. I don't know what my mom does.

*Do you have any brothers or sisters?*

I have a cat, Cinnamon. I feed him.

*Who cleans his litter box?*

Mom.

**John**
**11 years old**
**Boynton Beach, FL**

I go to see my grandparents a lot. They live in Lake Worth. They don't like any weird kinds of things. They think kids are too wild and everything. They're OK and all; it's just a pain to visit 'em, 'cause every time we go there I gotta take my earring out.

**Kevin**
**11 years old**
**Merrick, NY**

My mom and dad are divorced. My dad's remarried, and my mom's dating. The only think I can't take is when some of these guys come into the house and start telling me what to do. I mean, it's bad enough to have, like, strangers coming into the house. I know she needs to date. I don't want her to be lonely or anything, but she's gotta realize I might not like them, I might hate them. I'm not gonna like him just because she does. I'm not gonna call him "Dad" if they get married.

**Daryl**
**10 years old**
**Bristol, CT**

I was playing—throwing a ball around in the house—and I smashed my mom's big vase. It was real expensive, from China or something. My mom came down—I was standing there with all the pieces around me and water all over the place. She screamed at me for about five minutes, and then she sent me up to my room, and I couldn't come down all day.

*Did you want to come down?*

Nope.

**Debby**
**9 years old**
**Burlington, CT**

A lot of my relatives are dead already. Sometimes I go with my mom to visit my grandfather's grave. It's a little sad, but we plant flowers and everything.

I don't think old people are weird or anything, but sometimes they have diseases, or they might have something sticking out of their heads that makes them look weird, and then I wouldn't want to talk to them. . . . Yeah, my aunt had this brown thing growing on her forehead, and it got too big, so the doctors had to cut it off, but she died anyway.

# Art

**Leona**
**8 years old**
**Boca Raton, FL**

I'd give anything to meet the New Kids—the New Kids on the Block, the music group. There are so many things I'd like to ask them: How did you get started? Do you write your own music? But I don't think they do. They probably have some manager do that. I could spend a whole day with them without even talking and still enjoy it! I'd do *anything* to meet them.

**Kim**
**8 years old**
**James Beach, SC**

I love to watch TV.

*Have you caught on to this whole Teenage Mutant Ninja Turtles thing?*

Yeah, sorta. But, all the boys go crazy over it. They write about it in their school journals; they talk like it. I mean, I saw the movie and I thought it was OK—I like TMNT—but I *don't* want to talk about it *all* the time. That's the problem with boys.

**Jerry**
**8 years old**
**Minneapolis, MN**

I never watch television. I think all those shows are stupid. You've gotta be real stupid to like that stuff.

# Politics

**Rachel**
**9 years old**
**Hoboken, NJ**

*Would you like to spend a day with the president?*

No.

*What would you do if you* had *to spend a day with the president?*

I'd probably have to bring a whole bunch of puke bags. I didn't want Bush to be our president. I'm a Democrat. He's sort of weird, sort of whacko, you know what I mean? I wouldn't want to spend the day with him.

**Gale**
**14 years old**
**New Britain, CT**

I hate the whole animal-research thing. I understand that they have to kill some animals to research, like, AIDS; I don't understand how we can let them kill animals to find out about behavior, or pain—how much pain an animal can take—I saw some researchers doing that on a documentary. I think there are a lot of people who just like to kill animals.

**Denice**
**14 years old**
**Denver, CO**

I don't understand the whole right-to-die thing. Why don't they just let these people die? It's so stupid that people can't kill themselves if they want to. They have nothing to live for; they're in pain; they're a vegetable; they're paralyzed from the neck down; their families are suffering . . . how can the government tell people they have to go on like that?

**Leonard**
**13 years old**
**Denver, CO**

I don't agree with legalizing drugs. I think it would just make it easy for kids like me to get them. Letting people get drugs isn't the answer, the answer is getting people so that they don't want to use drugs.

**Mitch**
**14 years old**
**Twin Rivers, NJ**

I don't like this whole "Teachers are always right and kids are always wrong" thing. It's like a law. And it's no good, 'cause we're the leaders of tomorrow, and I don't think we get off to a good start when everybody tells us we're never right. I know we're right at least some of the times.

**Jeremiah**
**11 years old**
**Cambridge, MA**

I don't like it when my mom comes to school. Usually she'll go to the office and they'll call me down there, but sometimes she comes right to the classroom. One time I saw her in the window, out in the hall. I was like, "Oh no, what's going on here?" It's not right; it's embarrassing. Moms shouldn't just come into school like that. I mean, there are some things, you know . . . moms just shouldn't come into school like that.

**Seth**
**10 years old**
**Santa Monica, CA**

My mother cuts hair . . .

*Oh, she's a haircutter—*

No. She's a hairdresser. They're not the same. There's a big difference. A haircutter cuts hair the way the people want it. A hair designer designs hair—whatever's best for the person's hair. A dresser does 'em both. That's what my mom does. There's a big difference. If you said she cuts hair, she'd be all over you. She'd be screamin'.

# Fashion

**Linda**
**7 years old**
**Beverly Hills, CA**

Yesterday I cut up one of my pairs of jeans. My mom was all crazy, like, "That's a new pair of jeans!" I was like, "Mom, I got two other pairs of jeans; I think I can cut these up!" She just doesn't understand.

**Belinda**
**8 years old**
**Beverly Hills, CA**

Some of the kids in school really bug me. I mean, they wear the worst clothes—so stupid. There's a girl that sits next to me, and she wears the same thing every day.

**Rutger**
**12 years old**
**Charlotte, NC**

My father wears really ugly clothes. Really ugly. My mother always complains about it, 'cause she doesn't want to go out with him if he's wearing, like, a green blazer and a red tie. It's embarrassing.

# Education

**Jamie**
**15 years old**
**Lantana, FL**

We've got a big drug problem at our school. You can go up on the roof at any time during the day and do, or buy, any drug you want. Our school even has a drug-sniffing dog. He comes and inspects the lockers, but it doesn't do much good because everyone knows when he's coming, and they carry their stuff on them until he's gone. The dog can sniff the lockers but not the people.

**Rannie**
**16 years old**
**Venice Beach, CA**

Drugs are a part of high school. That's just the way it is, and it's not gonna change. High-school kids drink a lot; they smoke pot; they eat mushrooms—it's a part of life. In California you can't drink until you're 21, but everyone knows which liquor stores sell to minors, and a lot of kids have fake I.D.'s. You can get whatever you want. Kids use drugs for the same reasons adults do, and they get them almost as easily.

**Janice**
**13 years old**
**Los Angeles, CA**

Our teacher told us that you can't breathe the air in Los Angeles. So, like, what am I supposed to do?

**Darnel**
**13 years old**
**Bristol, CT**

I got left behind a grade because I don't read too good. I can't write too good. It kinda like runs in the family. My brother don't write too good either. My dad's a construction guy. He builds houses and stuff. I keep sayin', I'm gonna work for my dad so I don't have to worry 'bout writin' or nothin'. I just gotta know to use tools and stuff.

**Diane**
**9 years old**
**Boca Raton, FL**

I love television. I watch it all the time. "Cosby," "A Different World," "Full House." I could spend all day watching TV and never get bored. You can learn a lot from it too, lessons and stuff, that you can't learn in school.

**Stan**
**9 years old**
**Folly Island, SC**

I learn a lot about AIDS at home. I called the AIDS hotline, and they sent me a packet of stuff. I'm doing a report on it for school. I know about how you can get it, how you can't get it, how it is transmitted, how it attacks the immune system. I know what it is called: Acquired Immune Proficiency Syndrome. You'll probably die if you get it—not from the virus, from littler things you get because your immune system can't fight them.

I watched Ryan White on TV. He got it because he was a hemophiliac. Other people get it because they use needles; they're drug addicts. Homosexuals, they started it—prostitutes and stuff.

I think AIDS is the biggest problem in the world.

# History

**Rebeka**
**13 years old**
**Minneapolis, MN**

You know, Prince comes from Minneapolis. He still lives here. My godmother went to school with him. She said he didn't like to do any work at all. All he wanted to do was just play with his instruments. No work.

A lot of famous people came from Minnesota: Jessica Lange; Prince; Gretchen something, the Miss America from last year ("Minnesota girls are beautiful because we come from Sweden. Blond hair, blue eyes . . ."); Paul Molitor; Jill Trenary; that guy who walked across the snow (Will Steger, who completed a trek across Antarctica in March 1990); that fat guy, Louie Anderson. . . .

**Caryn**
**12 years old**
**Los Angeles, CA**

We're learning about the Boston Tea Party . . . well, something happened, and they didn't like it, and they went—they didn't wanna get it from them, 'cause they were like slavin' them and tellin' them what to do, and they were like, way across the country, so when the ship with the tea on it came in they like, blew it in the water . . .

**Reggie**
**11 years old**
**Boston, MA**

I got this report due in two days. We all have to write a report on some famous person. I'm doing it on Henry Mat . . . Madd . . . Mit . . . I can't remember what his name is. I guess I'll have to get some books or something. It's due in two days.

**Kevin**
**11 years old**
**Bristol, CT**

I think things were funnier a few years ago. Like, the old "Saturday Night Live" shows—they were much better than the new ones.

# Me

**Ernie**
**9 years old**
**Boca Raton, FL**

The thing that makes me special is I got bit in the face by a cat. It was injured, and I picked it up and started carryin' it home, and then it bit me in the face and jumped into the bushes. We never found it, so I had to get these shots. Five of 'em.

**Darren**
**11 years old**
**Charlotte, NC**

We gotta wear these uniforms to school: blue pants, white shirt, blue sweater, blue tie. We gotta wear it.

*What do you think about that?*

I think it sucks.

**Len**
**14 years old**
**West Windsor, NJ**

I've always been the kind of kid who gives 150 percent. I play three sports at school—soccer, baseball, football—and everybody knows they can count on me to play as good as I possibly can. That's why it hurt me when the whole Pete Rose scandal thing happened. My dad always called me Pete, because I tried so hard. I have all these Pete Rose posters on my bedroom walls. I turned them all over. I'll keep 'em that way until they let him back into baseball.

**Darcy**
**12 years old**
**Merrick, NY**

Call-waiting is a big problem for me. I talk on the phone for at least an hour and a half a night, and these men are always calling for my father when I'm on the phone. I put them on hold but my father says he's got to talk to them, so I never get to finish my calls. It happens *every* night.

**Lisa**
**8 years old**
**New Vernon, NJ**

I love horses. We have two horses and a pony here. I'm with them all the time.

> *What's special about horses? Why don't you love dogs instead?*

> *(Sardonically)* Well, you can't ride a dog.